$3.75

5/17/74

Glennon

FAMOUS FIGURES OF THE OLD TESTAMENT

Famous Figures of the Old Testament

By
WILLIAM JENNINGS BRYAN
Author of "In His Image," etc.

New York   Chicago
Fleming H. Revell Company
London   and   Edinburgh

New York: 158 Fifth Avenue
Chicago: 17 North Wabash Ave.
London: 21 Paternoster Square
Edinburgh: 75 Princes Street

In affectionate remembrance of John Baird, the revered father of my beloved wife, who, during a long period, beginning with his early conversion and ending only with his death at eighty-two, set a noble example by his high character, his consecrated life and his devotion to Christian work. His memory is a blessed heritage to his only child, and his grandchildren, who join in this loving dedication.

THIS volume offers to the public a number of brief sketches of famous figures in the Old Testament. Most of them were given originally as Bible Talks and are here brought together in book form at the request of numerous hearers with the hope that they will prove useful to Bible students in general and to teachers in particular.

Their publication also carries out a plan, which I have had in my mind for many years, of furnishing Sunday reading for Christians who, because of illness or advanced age, are denied the privilege of regular attendance at church services.

If I succeed in conveying to the minds and hearts of others the deep impression made upon myself by the study of these characters, my purpose will be accomplished.

W. J. B.

Miami, Florida.

Contents

9

I

ABRAHAM: THE HERO OF FAITH

GENESIS 12: 1-5; HEBREWS 11: 8-10, 17-19

FAITH is one of the trinity of virtues extolled by
Paul in his tribute to " faith, hope, charity."
No character in the Bible better illustrates it
than Abraham.

Two passages make this plain—one from Genesis,
which describes the call of Abraham, and one from
Hebrews, in which the Apostle recounts the faith of
the patriarch.

The story is briefly told, like all the wonderful stories
of the Bible. As literature they surpass in beauty, in
clearness, and in force all uninspired utterances.

" Now the Lord had said unto Abram, Get thee
out of thy country, and from thy kindred, and
from thy father's house, unto a land that I will shew
thee:

" And I will make of thee a great nation, and I will
bless thee, and make thy name great; and thou shalt be
a blessing:

" And I will bless them that bless thee, and curse him
that curseth thee: and in thee shall all families of the
earth be blessed.

" So Abram departed, as the Lord had spoken unto
him."

Where else can we find such an answer as this?

Here are two sentences embodied in a little more
than three verses. God spoke to Abram, setting forth

a promise as a reward for obedience, and " so Abram departed."

Where else can we find so great a communication so simply expressed? And where an answer that contained so much in so few words and meant so much to the human race?

God commanded; Abram obeyed; and mankind was blessed beyond the power of words to describe or figures to estimate.

It was a long journey in those days and into a strange land. Abram went with a purpose. He was to establish a family and a nation; his name was to be great and he was to be a blessing. He was seventy-five years old when the call came to him, but, nothing doubting, he gathered his substance together and all the family, including Lot, his brother's son, and they went forth into the land of Canaan.

" By faith, he obeyed."

Paul, in his great apostrophe to faith, says: " By faith, Abraham, when he was called to go out into a place which he should after receive for an inheritance, obeyed; and he went out, not knowing whither he went.

" By faith he sojourned in the land of promise, as in a strange country, dwelling in tabernacles [tents] with Isaac and Jacob, the heirs with him of the same promise.

" For he looked for a city which hath foundations, whose builder and maker is God."

First, a word as to the part which faith plays in human life. Much has been said about the relative importance of faith and works, but the discussion is of little practical value because neither is sufficient alone.

" Without faith it is impossible to please God,"

and, it may be added, impossible to do anything else of value.

Faith comes first and works afterward, but works must come. "Faith without works is dead." Believing comes before doing, but doing must follow.

Abraham believed God and, believing, obeyed.

How Abraham Aided and Was Aided.

If Abraham had had faith only—that is, faith without works—he would have been unknown because he would have done no work. He united the two and, by uniting them, proved what faith can accomplish when it expresses itself in the works to which faith leads.

Abraham established a family than which there has never been a greater. He also established a religion without which the family would have been unknown. The family for more than twenty centuries preserved the worship of one God and it may be just as truly said that religion also preserved the family.

When we speak of the aid which an individual renders to a great cause we sometimes overlook the fact that the cause gives more strength to those who support it than they can possibly give to the cause. A righteous cause has in it that which insures its triumph. Man can delay or hasten victory, but he cannot prevent victory and his contribution is often overestimated.

God uses those whom He chooses—fortunate are they unto whom He entrusts a great work. He selected Abram for this work, as He has selected others for particular tasks.

Exercise for the Imagination.

The Bible does not tell us why Abram was so favoured above others of his time. All we know is that

Abram was the son of Terah, who journeyed toward the land of Canaan as far as Haran, and died there.

Those who enjoy speculation can find ample exercise for the imagination in trying to picture the present condition of the world if Abram had not heard the voice of God calling him to his great work, or, hearing, had not obeyed.

Other races have appeared and disappeared; other nations have risen and fallen. Egypt once occupied the first place in the civilisation of her time. Archæologists still search for the riches buried in her splendid tombs.

Greece developed athletes with her national games, and her artists immortalised the perfection to which the body attained. Her philosophers, her orators, and her historians were for several centuries the leaders of the world.

The Only Thing That Lasts.

Then Rome rose to the height of her power and set the world's pace in law and in the science of war. Other nations have risen and impressed themselves upon history by some special line of work, but their superiority was not enduring.

Religion is the only thing that lasts. It made the Children of Israel a peculiar people and raised up such a host of great leaders as has never appeared among any other people of like number and opportunity.

Out of the race of Abraham and out of the monotheistic religion which he established came the Messiah Who, grafting Christianity upon Judaism, carried the religion of Abraham to every race and clime.

Beginning with the faith of one man, proven by his obedience, the worship of one God which he estab-

lished, interpreted and fulfilled by Christ, has become
the greatest pillar of strength to the mightiest nations
of the earth and the hope of the world.

Our Ruling Element.

And what lesson does this bring to us?

First, that faith is the ruling element in our own
lives.

It is faith that gives us whatever strength we have
and leads us to the accomplishment of all that we do.

In order that we may feel physically equal to the
tasks that are before us, we seek to make our bodies
strong to endure fatigue and to resist disease.

In order to meet successfully the problems of life, we
train our mental faculties and store our minds with
useful information.

We know that consciousness of preparedness gives
us that confidence in our powers which is necessary to
success.

We know, too, that faith in the righteousness of our
purpose is necessary to give us the fortitude that we
need for large undertakings.

Shakespeare declares that "thrice is he armed that
hath his quarrel just"; the Bible puts it much more
strongly when it says that one with God shall chase a
thousand, and two put ten thousand to flight.

Greatest Need of All.

No one can accomplish much by himself, he must
work with others; and to work with others, he must
have faith in his fellow men.

It is better to have faith in one's fellows and be deceived occasionally than to distrust everyone.

Christ took weak men and made them strong; He

took doubting men and made them confident; He took timid men and made them courageous; He had faith in the common people and they rewarded His trust by hearing Him gladly.

So we must be able to see beyond superficial differences and find similarity in the deep running currents of life.

People who differ from us are quite likely to be as honest as we are. Reasoning together wipes out misunderstandings and, by revealing unity of purpose, secures unity of action.

Faith in God is the greatest need—to this the Christian adds faith in the Bible as the Word of God and faith in Christ as Son of God and Saviour of the world.

But as faith in the Bible and faith in Christ rest upon faith in God, we come back to the greatest of all thoughts, the thought of God, and to the greatest of all facts, the fact of God. We cannot hear His voice unless we listen, and we will not listen unless we believe in Him.

The Call That Comes to All.

The second lesson is that of obedience.

God's call comes to all—each is summoned to a duty for which he is fitted, or can be fitted, and to a work which is within his power.

The ministry is spoken of as a calling because the minister feels that God calls him to consecrate his entire life to God's work.

He prepares himself by study and renews his strength constantly by prayer. Because his whole heart and his whole mind are absorbed in the preaching of the Gospel, he is able to present the truths of God's Word with the maximum of effectiveness.

But this does not excuse the layman from responding to the calls that come to him. The Heavenly Father has work for all, and to those who are anxious to hear and willing to heed, He will point out the things that need to be done.

We can all aid in making the city in which we live like the city which Abraham sought—one " whose builder and maker is God."

Those who are ready to obey will not have to wait long for a commission. God's employment bureau has jobs for all.

God's Promises Fulfilled.

The third lesson is that God's promises are more than fulfilled.

As Abram, afterwards raised to Abraham, could not conceive of the magnitude of the work to which God called him, so we are not able to calculate the importance of the work that we are called to do.

If we are instrumental in saving but one soul, we become a partner in all the good that that one soul may accomplish thereafter.

A word of encouragement may seem like a trivial thing at the time, and yet it may echo throughout eternity.

It seems a wonderful thing to be able to stand by the side of a telegraph instrument and speak to people who are ten thousand miles away, but the heart can do more than that—it can speak to hearts that will beat ten thousand years after all our hearts are still .

Abraham still speaks to us through the religion that he established, and so we, if God deigns to speak through us, may communicate His message throughout succeeding generations.

II

JOSEPH: THE DREAMER

GENESIS 45: 3-15

THE story of Joseph is one of the most fascinating ever written.

Even from the standpoint of literary excellence it is unsurpassed and its value is infinitely increased because it is a matter of history and also because of the many moral lessons which it teaches.

Its truthfulness is so apparent that it carries conviction with it.

Jacob had two wives, Leah and Rachel, besides his slave wives. Leah was imposed upon him; after he had worked seven years for Rachel, his father-in-law insisted that he take Leah first because she was the elder; so he worked seven years more to get the woman whom he loved.

Therefore, his partiality for Joseph and Benjamin, the children of Rachel, was not unnatural. Neither was the jealousy of the other brothers unnatural. It is not unlikely that they would have been jealous had they been full brothers instead of half-brothers.

The Bible's Trustworthiness.

It is not necessary to commend the father for manifesting his special affection for Joseph; he might have known it would have aroused antagonism among the other sons. But parents are not always wise in this respect. The Bible is the more to be trusted because it describes Bible characters as they were, with their follies—even their sins—mixed with their virtues.

But Joseph himself was innocently responsible for a third cause of irritation. He was a dreamer and indiscreetly told his dreams to his brothers.

He was too young to understand the importance of keeping to himself a revelation of the supremacy that was to come to him. He may have but faintly realised the significance of his dreams and was entirely ignorant of the wonderful career that they foreshadowed.

The brothers, with three reasons for hostility, plotted to get rid of him.

The Hand of Providence.

Here the hand of Providence begins to manifest itself. Those who are selected and prepared for a great work are also guarded against harm—even directed by mysterious ways to the accomplishment of God's purpose.

" Come, let us slay him," said some of his brethren. Killing is such an easy way of getting rid of one who stands in the way—many monarchs have played at this game—and yet, those always fail who try to dispose of one to whom God has entrusted a task. The truth for which the hated one stands not only survives him, but is often aided by the shedding of martyr blood.

Reuben appears just at the crititcal moment—there is always a Reuben about in such crises—and suggested that they save themselves the guilt of murder by putting Joseph down into a pit which was conveniently near.

Reuben's intentions were good; he expected to rescue Joseph and deliver him to his father again. But, fortunately for Joseph, fortunately for his brethren, and fortunately for Egypt, Reuben's rescue plans miscarried.

A " Happy " Solution.

While he was away some Ishmaelitish merchants passed by and Judah, who had an eye to business as well as a little awakening of conscience, suggested that they sell Joseph. The other brothers consented to what seemed a happy solution of the difficulty; they would get rid of their dreamer brother and yet escape responsibility for his death.

So they fixed up a deception for the father and settled down to enjoy their emancipation from companionship with the object of their dislike.

The father accepted their account of his son's death —convinced by the kid's blood into which they had dipped the " coat of many colours "—and mourned Joseph's death. All went well until a famine came into the land; then it became necessary for Jacob to send his sons down into Egypt to buy some corn and there they found the dreamer—and he had the corn. It is not bad to be a dreamer—if you have the corn when it is needed.

The Invisible Armour of Character.

In the meantime, Joseph was making history himself.

The character that had been built up and established in the home of his father continued to be his priceless possession. His brothers could take from him his coat; they could sell him away from his home and make him a slave in a strange land, but his character was beyond the reach of their evil designs.

It was the invisible armour which enmity could not pierce—it could even blunt the darts of passion and keep him unharmed in the presence of the most trying of temptations. He preferred the dungeon to a betrayal of his trust and surrender of his integrity—little knowing that the place by the side of Pharaoh could not be reached by any other route than that which led through the prison.

Here is where the reason breaks down and faith becomes the only reliable guide. No one can reason out a course like that which Joseph followed; one must have faith to do the right, regardless of consequences, and leave the rest with God.

The Riddle of Dreams.

It was a fellow-prisoner who brought to Joseph an opportunity for service which all of his brethren could not have offered him. Two men with dreams told their dreams to a chance companion who happened to be a dreamer and an interpreter of dreams. God had not only given Joseph two prophetic dreams, but He had given him the power to understand dreams.

Who can solve the riddle of the dream? Many theories have been proposed in explanation of dreams, nearly all of which attempt to rob them of any special significance or power. Those who believe the Bible need not be distressed if such explanations prove unsatisfactory; the Bible explanation of dreams is sufficient.

The God who can speak to man in the daytime can communicate with him also at night. The sun never goes down on the Creator's power; there is no hiatus in His relationship to His children.

"Within the shadow" ever stands the Unseen Power that can give strength to resolution in times that try men's souls; this same Power can make the dream as vivid at night as the vision is at mid-day.

The Use of Unfermented Wine.

Two of the prisoners had dreams; one of them Joseph interpreted to mean death and the other life.

I hope my readers will pardon me for calling attention to the fact that the dream of Pharaoh's chief butler gives us high authority for the use of unfermented wine. This is the language of the butler:

"In my dream, behold, a vine was before me; and in the vine were three branches; and it was as though it budded, and her blossoms shot forth; and the clusters thereof brought forth ripe grapes; and Pharaoh's cup was in my hand; and I took the grapes, and pressed them into Pharaoh's cup, and I gave the cup into Pharaoh's hand."

No fermentation there—no alcohol, just the juice fresh from the grape.

The dream was a prophecy, and it meant life to the dreamer.

"Then Pharaoh Called Joseph."

The hand of Providence appears again. Pharaoh had a dream and that dream was repeated with a different illustration of the fact that it represented. Nobody could interpret the dream.

Now re-enters the butler upon the scene. He had a chance to pay his debt to Joseph and at the same time to help the king. So, even though it required the re-calling of his own wrong-doing, he told of Joseph and of his power to interpret dreams.

"Then Pharaoh sent and called Joseph." It does not say whether they put him into prison slowly, but it does say that they "brought him hastily out of the dungeon."

The dreamer was ready to enter upon his work; all the rest had been preparation. He listened to Pharaoh's dream and, with the power that God gave him, he disclosed the meaning thereof.

Joseph's Great Opportunity.

There were to be seven years of plenty and then seven years of famine. As in the dream the poor kine ate up the fat kine, and the thin ears devoured the full ears, so the years of famine would consume all that was grown in the years of plenty.

But Joseph's wisdom went beyond the interpretation of the dream. He ventured to advise Pharaoh; he told him now to protect his land from the famine by the conservation of the food in the years of plenty through the employment of "a man discreet and wise." It is not strange that Pharaoh chose as the "man discreet and wise," suggested by Joseph, the man "in whom the spirit of God is."

Thus God led Joseph into a great opportunity after He had prepared him to meet the responsibilities of such a position. In a multitude of cases the hand of God has been as clearly manifest.

If this is true in the writing of great pages of history, what reason have we to doubt that God's hand leads in writing pages less conspicuous? Who is able to draw a line through human events and declare what is worth God's while or when the situation is important enough for Him to have a part in the direction of men's lives?

Our text gives us the sequel; Joseph, in power over all Egypt, revealed himself to his brethren, seeking to buy food from Pharaoh because the famine was sore in Canaan also; and they, conscience stricken, felt that judgment was about to be rendered against them for their sins. But Joseph relieved their fears and calmed their agitation.

"Be not grieved, nor angry with yourselves, that ye sold me hither; for God did send me before you to preserve life."

It was God's work—"He maketh the wrath of man to praise Him."

Man is free to choose his course; he must be free if he is to be held accountable for his doings. But God is free to use the wicked as well as the good to execute His plans.

If man will sin, let him do so—it is his privilege. But he must not complain at the punishment that God fixes and he should not be surprised at the ways of escape which God provides.

God's Extended Hand.

We draw from this a lesson that is daily needed and wonderfully helpful. God keeps watch above His own; those who trust Him cannot fail.

The way may be dark and the perils great, but the God who sent Joseph on before "to preserve a remnant in the earth" and to save his brethren "by a great deliverance" is equal to any task.

He is bigger than the world that He has made and is all-loving as well as all-powerful. Our lives are precious in His sight; His hand is extended; He will lead us if we put our trust in Him.

III

MOSES: THE LAWGIVER

EXODUS 10: 13-22

MOSES reached the highest place to which any human being has attained. He was entrusted with a great task and, talking with God and walking with God, acquitted himself nobly.

No one has given more conclusive proof of what God can do with a human being who surrenders himself to divine guidance and becomes His spokesman.

Moses was born of an obscure family, the son of a mother who, either by supernatural suggestion or by remarkable prevision, saved her child from a cruel king's decree.

Providence or extraordinary chance brought the child into the household of the very sovereign who had plotted against his life—the heart of the king's daughter being touched by the crying of the infant in the bullrushes.

Thus a man was saved for a great work and prepared for his task as he could not have been prepared in any other way.

An Important Test.

When he reached manhood's estate he was tested, and a very important test it was.

Had he been spoiled by his environment; had he been weaned away from his race by the allurements

of the court, he would not have been a fit person to
lead the Children of Israel out of bondage.

But his anger betrayed his kinship and proved that
his sympathies were with his oppressed brethren. He
cast aside the riches that might have been his, and the
power and prestige that association with royalty would
have brought him, and was true to the ties that bound
him to his race.

I digress a moment to emphasise a very important
fact; namely, that the heart directs the life and determines one's fitness for service.

The learning that Moses had acquired and the intellectual power he had developed could not alone have
made him the leader that he was. Had his heart been
with the Egyptians, he might have been put in command of his brethren and whipped them to their daily
toil. All of his mission and intellect would have been
as obedient to his heart had he taken the side of
Pharaoh.

Because he was in heart and in sympathy one of
them, he pitied the sufferings of his people and hated
those who ruled them with a cruel rod.

Moses' Call to Service.

The second period of his life opened with the call
that came to him as he tended Jethro's flocks in Midian.
His attention was drawn to a bush that burned and yet
was not consumed; he drew near and heard the Voice
that directed his life from that day.

The materialists, limiting themselves to the information that comes through the senses, cannot understand how there could have been a burning bush or a
voice emanating from it.

They are egotistical enough to put their lack of understanding against the facts of history and the accomplishments of this great Bible hero, in spite of the fact that myriads since that day have been called to the service of God—called by a voice distinct enough to make those who heard it willing to stake their lives upon it.

Every great task, accomplished through sacrifice, has back of it a call audible to the person summoned. How else can we explain the courage of the martyrs and the patience of the saints?

"Who Hath Made Man's Mouth?"

Moses was modest; he distrusted his ability to do the work committed to him.

"O my Lord," he protested, "I am not eloquent, neither heretofore, nor since thou hast spoken unto thy servant: but I am slow of speech, and of a slow tongue."

Behold the reproof: "Who hath made man's mouth? . . . have not I, the Lord? Now, therefore, go, and I will be with thy mouth, and teach thee what thou shalt say."

Blessed is the man through whom the Lord speaks. He who can give life a purpose and fill the heart with zeal can also supply the tongue with the language that will best express the thought to be conveyed.

The Lord selected Aaron as a prophet to Moses—as an adjutant to make known the leader's instructions. But experience showed that the brother was not a second Moses or at all comparable with him.

Aaron shines by the light of Moses and reflects that light very imperfectly. He did not walk as close to God as Moses did.

Then follows the story of a people's release from
bondage with miracles wrought and plagues suffered—
a record so familiar that it need not be recounted here.

Just two thoughts in passing. Pharaoh set succeeding despots an example which they have not been slow
to follow. When the Israelites complained of the
severity of their overseers their tasks were increased.

" Bricks without straw " has passed into the language of all nations as the most forcible description of
requirements that are excessive, and the result is ever
the same.

Instead of silencing complaint, increased severity
furnishes the stimulus necessary to deliverance.
Cruelty brings about a reaction that counts in the final
conflict and gives victory to the right.

The Heavenly Father is not so far away from us
but that He can hear the pleadings of those who
suffer.

Tragedy That Brings Advancement.

The second thought is found in the tenth plague, the
killing of the first-born. The tragedy of death seems
to be the only thing that can remedy a great wrong.

Vicarious suffering is not a strange thing; it is the
central thing in the advancement of civilisation. Important reforms seldom come until the shedding of
innocent blood has aroused thought and stirred to
action the forces that insure the progress of the race.

Our text takes up the story after Pharaoh had been
humbled and had not only released the Children of
Israel but had sent them on their way; afterwards he
changed his mind and started in pursuit of the fleeing
Israelites.

We find them in the first of their many exhibitions of weakness.

After God had delivered them by wonderful manifestations of power and finally by a token of favouritism that was made the basis of the Feast of the Passover, observed throughout the centuries, " they were sore afraid "; " they cried out unto the Lord."

The Miracle at the Red Sea.

Moses began at this time his series of remonstrances with them for their lack of faith. " Fear ye not, stand still, and see the salvation of the Lord, which he will show to you today; for the Egyptians whom ye have seen today, ye shall see them again no more for ever."

We are here again told of the " pillar of the cloud by day " and " the pillar of fire by night " which stood between the Children of Israel and the Egyptians until Moses stretched out his hand over the sea as he was commanded.

God " caused the sea to go back by a strong east wind all that night, and made the sea dry land, and the waters were divided."

Here again the materialists are disturbed; they try to account for the deliverance of the Children of Israel without giving credit to a supernatural agency.

The text says that God " caused the sea to go back," using as an agency " a strong east wind " that blew " all that night."

Why Not Believe?

If the text read that " It so happened that an east wind chanced to blow just at that particular time," the materialists could believe it; why not believe that the God, who made the seas and fixed their boundaries, who created the winds and gave unto them the laws by which they are governed, and also created man and assigned to him his work—why not believe that such a God could use such a wind at such a time to open a way through such a sea for His supreme handiwork—man?

Those who prefer to worship chance rather than God will be compelled to overtax their imagination when they try to explain why the Children of Israel went through the sea on dry ground while the waters overwhelmed the pursuing Egyptians.

However, the escape from Pharaoh and his overseers was just the beginning of the experiences of the people whom Moses led.

They were hardly out of one difficulty before they were into another.

Still They Found Fault.

They scarcely rose from their knees after an expression of gratitude before they raised their voices in complaint.

They had waters from the smitten rock at Meribah, and manna in the wilderness, but still they found fault.

They passed through all degrees of enthusiasm, from ecstasy in the hours of triumph to the worship of a golden calf when Moses was for a short time absent from them.

Moses, the liberator, was also Moses the lawgiver. The commandments which he brought down from Sinai are a fundamental part of the world's thought today.

It is interesting to compare the " Thou Shalt Not's " of these commandments with the modern statutes based upon them. The laws written upon the tables of stone were simple, clear, and easily understood.

Take the two that are paraphrased in the legislation of all lands, "Thou shalt not kill," and "Thou shalt not steal." Each is stated in a sentence with four words and each word has but one syllable. Another commandment has five words and still another six.

Moses' Story of Creation.

In one sentence of ten words—"In the beginning God created the heaven and the earth"—Moses gives the only history of creation which has stood the test of time; was it human wisdom or inspiration?

In one sentence, "And God said, Let the earth bring forth the living creature after his kind," he announced God's universal law governing the continuity of life upon this earth.

In still another sentence, "Let us make man in our image," he gives the only explanation of the riddle of life—the only reason for man's presence in the world.

Speaking as God gave him utterance, he formulated a code of laws and a system of rules for a chosen people—laws and rules that comprehended all their needs.

After his work was finished and his followers ready to take possession of the promised land, he disappeared and "no man knoweth of his sepulchre."

Law Giver Without a Peer.

Somewhere in the land of Moab, near Mount Nebo, he resigned his body to the dust from which it came and committed his soul to God.

He rose, as the sun seems to rise, from the dead level; he ascended, as the sun seems to ascend, to meridian splendour; and then he descended, as the sun seems to descend, to the level from which he started.

Leader beyond comparison—lawgiver without a peer.

IV

JOSHUA: THE OPTIMIST

WE hear, today, a great deal of the optimist and
the pessimist, and read definitions of both
that cover a wide range. Joshua may be ap-
propriately described as an optimist in the highest and
best sense of that word. He was not an optimist in
the sense that many are today, believing that everything
will be all right, but trusting that others will do whatever needs to be done; neither was he such an optimist
as those who refuse to see anything but the bright side
and therefore overlook dangers in the way and ob-
stacles that must be overcome. He took his stand on
God's side, reckoned accurately as to the forces that
had to be met and then went to work with a perfect
faith, relying for help upon One with whom all things
are possible. That is true optimism.

One of the Appointed Spies

While he appeared in an important undertaking some
years before, we can commence our narrative with his
appointment by Moses as one of the commission sent
to spy out Canaan when the Children of Israel came
near to the Promised Land. He was of the tribe of
Ephraim and the son of Nun. His name was Oshea
until Moses gave him the name of Jehoshua, or Joshua,
as he was better known. The spies reached Canaan
" at the time of the first ripe grapes." They spent

ıorty days examining the land which had been given them and carried back with them a cluster of grapes so large that "they bare it between two upon a staff." The picture of this huge bunch of grapes is familiar to all Sunday School children.

The twelve spies joined in a report which represented Canaan as a land that "floweth with milk and honey." The grapes, together with pomegranates and figs, were exhibited as specimens of the fruit of the land. Thus far all the spies were agreed, but were the Children of Israel strong enough to take possession of the land? Upon this proposition the twelve were divided; ten lacked faith and were frightened by the inhabitants of the land promised to the Children of Israel. They said:

" Nevertheless the people be strong that dwell in the land, and the cities are walled, and very great: and moreover we saw the children of Anak there.

" The Amalekites dwell in the land of the south: and the Hittites, and the Jebusites, and the Amorites, dwell in the mountains: and the Canaanites dwell by the sea, and by the coast of Jordan " (Num. 13: 28, 29).

Caleb and Joshua Confident.

Caleb and Joshua, two of the twelve, were confident of the superior strength of the Children of Israel and favoured an immediate advance into the land. Upon the question of ability to conquer the inhabitants, Caleb and Joshua presented a minority report and it created a great stir in the camp—such a stir as a minority report sometimes creates in a political convention or a religious assembly. Great reforms, it may be added, usually begin in a minority report.

Caleb, speaking for himself and Joshua, " stilled the

people before Moses, and said, Let us go up at once, and possess it; for we are well able to overcome it.

" But the men that went up with him said, We be not able to go up against the people; for they are stronger than we.

" And they brought up an evil report of the land which they had searched unto the children of Israel, saying, The land, through which we have gone to search it, is a land that eateth up the inhabitants thereof; and all the people that we saw in it are men of great stature.

" And there we saw the giants, the sons of Anak, which come of the giants; and we were in our own sight as grasshoppers, and so we were in their sight " (Num. 13 : 30-33).

The whole congregation was excited and " cried; and the people wept that night." The Children of Israel murmured against Moses and against Aaron "— as they had often done—" and the whole congregation said unto them :

" Would God that we had died in the land of Egypt! or would God we had died in this wilderness!

" And wherefore hath the Lord brought us unto this land, to fall by the sword, that our wives and our children should be a prey? were it not better for us to return into Egypt? " (Num. 14 : 1-3).

They even said one to another, " Let us make a captain, and let us return into Egypt." It must have been discouraging to Moses to hear these taunts and insults after so many wonderful evidences of God's love and power. His patience was tested as sorely as was the patience of Job—he certainly deserved the description that the Lord gave of him :

" Now the man Moses was very meek, above all

the men which were upon the face of the earth "
(Num. 12:3).

The Children of Israel had quenched their thirst
with the water that flowed from a smitten rock; they
had gathered manna from the ground and they had
feasted on quail sent especially for their table. They
had been guided by a pillar of fire by night and a pillar
of cloud by day. Time and time again they had found
God's strength sufficient for them—and still they
complained.

It was at this point that Joshua stepped forward and
tried to infuse into the Children of Israel the confidence
that made his own heart strong. But his words did
not convince the unappreciative and ungrateful people
to whom they were addressed; " but all the congregation bade stone them with stones." Then follows the
Lord's rebuke and the successful plea of Moses in their
behalf—that is, successful in securing entrance into the
Promised Land, delayed until after those guilty of rebellion had passed away.

Successor of Moses.

When Moses was about to lay down his mighty task
he, under the direction of the Almighty, selected Joshua
as his successor. In the first chapter of Joshua we are
told that the Lord spake unto Joshua, the son of Nun,
and said unto him, " Go over this Jordan, and all this
people, unto the land which I do give to them, even to
as I said unto Moses."

Joshua immediately called his officers together and
had them prepare the people to march within three days.
The first miracle performed under his leadership stayed
your foot shall tread upon, that have I given unto you,
the children of Israel. Every place that the sole of

the waters of the Jordan and enabled the Children of Israel to pass over dry-shod. His second victory was the capture of Jericho. The following is the plan as set forth in the sixth chapter of Joshua:

" And the Lord said unto Joshua, See, I have given into thine hand Jericho, and the king thereof, and the mighty men of valour.

" And ye shall compass the city, all ye men of war, and go round about the city once. Thus shalt thou do six days.

" And seven priests shall bear before the ark seven trumpets of rams' horns: and the seventh day ye shall compass the city seven times, and the priests shall blow with the trumpets.

" And it shall come to pass, that when they make a long blast with the ram's horn, and when ye hear the sound of the trumpet, all the people shall shout with a great shout; and the wall of the city shall fall down flat, and the people shall ascend up every man straight before him."

The Taking of Jericho.

Joshua did as he was commanded; the priests and the people encircled the city six times—once a day for six successive days; on the seventh day when the trumpets were sounded Joshua said unto the people: " Shout, for the Lord hath given you the city, and the people shouted with a great shout and the wall fell down flat so that the people went into the city, every man straight before him and they took the city."

The miracle, when analysed, presents but three questions: First: Can God perform a miracle? He can, if He is God. A Creator, such as God is believed to be, all-wise, all-powerful, and all-loving, can do anything

He wills to do—"With God all things are possible."
It may be that a miracle is the result of forces in nature
not yet known to man—forces that overcome the forces
that he does know, as the electric current and the radio
overcome space, but not necessarily so. We cannot set
bounds to God's power or put limits upon Him. To
deny that God *can* perform a miracle is to deny that
God is God.

Second: Would God want to perform a miracle?
That is the real question that troubles some, but it only
troubles those who think themselves able to know without possibility of mistake what God would want to do
—an assumption that raises the one who makes it to
the level of God Himself or brings God down to man's
level. What mind, unless it be infinite in its grasp, can
know with certainty what an Infinite Mind would wish
to do?

Asking pardon for using an illustration first used by
me nearly a quarter of a century ago, I reproduce the
following extract from " The Prince of Peace ":

I was eating a piece of watermelon some months ago and
was struck with its beauty. I took some of the seed and
weighed them, and found that it would require some five
thousand seed to weigh a pound. And then I applied mathematics to a forty-pound melon. One of these seeds, put into
the ground, when warmed by the sun and moistened by the
rain goes to work; it gathers from somewhere two hundred
thousand times its own weight and, forcing this raw material through a tiny stem, constructs a watermelon. It
covers the outside with a coating of green; inside of the
green it puts a layer of white, and within the white a core of
red, and all through the red it scatters seeds, each one
capable of continuing the work of reproduction. I cannot
explain the watermelon, but I eat it and enjoy it. Everything that grows tells a like story of infinite power. Why

should I deny that a divine hand fed a multitude with a few loaves and fishes when I see hundreds of millions fed every year by a hand which converts the seeds scattered over the field into an abundant harvest? We know that food can be multiplied in a few months' time, shall we deny the power of the Creator to eliminate the element of time, when we have gone so far in eliminating the element of space?

Third: Did God actually perform the miracle? This question is easily answered in the affirmative by those who answer the first and second questions in the affirmative. It is needless to submit the third question to those who answer the first or second in the negative. The evidence is sufficient to convince those who do not exclude the miracle as an impossibility. It was believed by those who lived at the time and it has been believed by thousands of millions who have lived since. When we consider that the Lord of Hosts was in charge of the attack on Jericho—the Lord who raised up prophets and, through them, shaped the destiny of nations,— overthrowing armies and giving victory to His chosen people—all for the purpose of carrying out a divine plan—why should we question the possibility, the probability, or the actuality of such a victory as was won by Joshua when, at the command of the Almighty, he led the Children of Israel into the land that God had selected for them.

It is unnecessary to follow Joshua as, step by step, he conducted the Children of Israel, driving out and destroying wicked peoples to make a place for those who were to convert Jerusalem into a great religious centre from which the worship of one God would radiate to every part of the world.

Joshua's methods of warfare have often been made the subject of condemnation by agnostics and infidels.

The killing of men, women and children is not a thing easily defended; it might be if we knew all the facts. A court does not feel itself qualified to render judgment until both sides are heard. Those who are most quick to set up a standard of justice of their own and to condemn the Almighty for falling below this standard— for Joshua carried out specific instructions from the Lord Himself—happen to be the very ones who exalt Nature and profess to reverence Nature alone. And yet, Nature is infinitely more cruel than God has ever been represented as being. The sea and the floods do not spare men, women or children, neither do the winds and the flames. Ask the earthquake to number its dead and the volcanoes to count their victims. What sympathy has the plague? What pity has the pestilence? And who will justify the cruel delusions of the mirage? When we have satisfied ourselves as to the *why* of the death-dealing visitations of inanimate forces—and not until then—will we be wise enough to call Jehovah to account for the manner in which He exterminated wicked nations and substituted the adoration of Himself for the worship of idols. If God is to be condemned for the cruelties which He commands, how shall we excuse Him for the cruelties caused by the laws that He has imposed upon Nature? Criticism of God leads logically to a denial of the very existence of God. If we have too little information to enable us to *commend,* surely we have too little to justify us in condemning.

Joshua justified the confidence placed in him. He established Israel in the land of promise; his strength did not fail him until his work was accomplished.

His last act was to call together the elders, judges, officers and people and to deliver unto them an eloquent

exhortation. He reminded them that it was the Lord
their God who had fought for them, and said:

" Be ye therefore very courageous to keep and to do
all that is written in the book of the law of Moses, that
ye turn not aside therefrom to the right hand or to the
left " (Chap. 23: 6).

The Test of a Leader.

The test of a leader is to be found in the impression
that he makes upon his followers and in the kind of
men he gathers around him. Israel not only served the
Lord all the days of Joshua, but " all the days of the
elders that outlived Joshua." His optimism pervaded
the nation; he believed in the triumph of righteousness
because God stands back of the right with an arm
strong enough to bring victory to his side, and he
communicated his faith to his people. He accomplished
the work unto which he was called, never faltering for
a moment. Opposition did not discourage him because
he relied upon a God as infinite in power as in wisdom
and in love.

V

GIDEON: THE MAN WHO OBEYED AND WON

JUDGES 6-8

CINCINNATUS, the great Roman who was twice called from the plough to guide the destiny of his nation, left a name which, for two thousand years, has been given to farmers who have been summoned by their countrymen to perform great patriotic tasks. But Cincinnatus was not the first farmer to be so called. The Roman lived about five hundred years before Christ; three hundred years earlier, Amos left his herd of goats and the care of sycamore trees to assume the rôle of a prophet of Israel in the days when the luxury of the rich was rotting away the foundations of Israel. A hundred years before this, Elisha left his plough standing in the furrow to receive the mantle which fell from Elijah when the latter ascended in a chariot of fire.

A Thresher of Wheat.

But more than three hundred years before Elisha's day, Gideon left the threshing of wheat to undertake the deliverance of the Children of Israel from the Midianites, and became the fifth of the Judges of Israel. As has often occurred since, the farmers were at that time the victims of injustice. The marauding Midianites would sweep down upon the

fields of the Hebrews and carry away their crops.
The suffering was very great and the people were in
despair.

In the sixth chapter of the Book of Judges we read
that there " came an angel of the Lord, and sat under
an oak which was in Ophrah, that pertained unto Joash
the Abiezrite: and his son Gideon threshed wheat by
the winepress, to hide it from the Midianites. And the
angel of the Lord appeared unto him, and said unto
him, The Lord is with thee, thou mighty man of
valour."

Gideon had an enquiring mind and he put a question
to the angel: " Oh, my Lord," he said, " if the Lord be
with us, why then is all this befallen us? and where be
all his miracles which our fathers told us of, saying,
Did not the Lord bring us up from Egypt? but now the
Lord hath forsaken us, and delivered us into the hands
of the Midianites."

The Lord answered him with a commission: " Go in
this thy might, and thou shalt save Israel from the hand
of the Midianites: have not I sent thee? "

But Gideon was modest as well as brave and pleaded:
" Oh, my Lord, wherewith shall I save Israel? behold,
my family is poor in Manasseh, and I am the least in
my father's house."

In this depreciation of himself, he was quite different
from the Roman Cincinnatus, who was a patrician.

Then the angel performed a miracle which, while
it deeply impressed Gideon, was not quite enough to
give him full confidence in his call. He had faith
enough, however, to accomplish the first task assigned
to him, the overthrowing of the altar to Baal which his
own father had erected, and the cutting down of the
grove that stood by it. He was timid enough, however,

to do the work at night because he feared his father's household and the men of the city—but he did it.

"And when the men of the city arose early in the morning, behold, the altar of Baal was cast down, and the grove was cut down, that was by it, and the second bullock was offered upon the altar that was built." This was equivalent to a declaration of war and the Midianites and the Amalekites prepared for battle.

A Sign Given to Gideon of the Lord.

Then follows the familiar sign which God gave him, the fleece of wool that was wet with dew while all the earth around it was dry. Not quite convinced yet, he asked that the earth should be wet with dew and the fleece be left dry. This was done, and it was enough to convince Gideon that he was chosen for the work assigned him and he proceeded to put his forces in battle array.

Then came that wonderful proof of God's power and of man's faith that has rendered the name of Gideon immortal. The Christian traveling men of the United States have given his name to their very useful organization. One of its accomplishments has been to put Bibles in the rooms of the hotels of the country.

The Lord told Gideon that he had too many men, that the number must be reduced, "lest Israel vaunt themselves, saying that their own hand hath saved them," although they had only thirty-two thousand as against an enemy that "lay along in the valley like grasshoppers for multitude and their camels were without number, like the sand of the sea for multitude." Under instructions from the Almighty, Gideon asked all who were fearful and afraid to depart from Mount Gilead. Twenty-two thousand availed themselves of the opportunity to retire, leaving but ten thousand men. "And the Lord said unto Gideon, The people are yet too many," and he was asked to select from his reduced army those that "lapped of the water with the tongue, as a dog lappeth." This has been construed as a test; some of the soldiers scooped up water as they ran, while others deliberately got down on their knees to drink. Only three hundred men stood this last test, and the remaining nine thousand seven hundred were dismissed for the time being. Then Gideon, the farmer-general, led his little band of three hundred against the unnumbered opponents, encouraged by a dream which one of the enemy had, indicating the defeat of the Midianites. Gideon divided his three hundred men into three companies, giving to each man a trumpet, an empty pitcher, and a lamp within the pitcher. They were commanded to watch him and do as he did. At a signal to be given by him, they were to blow the trumpets, break the pitchers and shout, "The sword of the Lord and of Gideon!"—not the sword of Gideon and of the Lord, or the sword of Gideon alone, but "The sword of the Lord and of Gideon."

"If God Be For Us, Who Can Be Against Us?"

His little band was faithful to a man. They surrounded the camp and, at the signal, revealed their lights and cried, "The sword of the Lord and of Gideon!" They did their part and the enemy "ran and cried and fled." The Lord did His part, also, which was to "set every man's sword against his fellow." Then the rest of the army took part and slew the fleeing Midianites.

An impossible story? It might seem so if only human power had engaged in the conflict, but when the

God of Battles is in command three hundred soldiers are quite enough. He could bring fear into the hearts of the enemy and, to frightened men three hundred trumpets would sound like as many thousand, while three hundrel lamps would make them think that all the stars of heaven had fallen down upon them. A broken pitcher, plus God, is mightier than a two-edged sword in the hands of a man.

The Israelites were very grateful to Gideon for delivering them from their enemies—so grateful that they said unto him, " Rule thou over us, both thou and thy son, and thy son's son also." But Gideon said, " I will not rule over you, neither shall my son rule over you; the Lord shall rule over you." A noble sentiment—and the last noble sentiment recorded of him. While he would not accept the authority that they offered to bestow upon him, he asked each man to give him the earrings of his prey, and they did so. The earrings totalled in weight a thousand and seven hundred shekels of gold, not to speak of other ornaments. Gideon made an ephod of the gold and put it in his home city and it " became a snare unto Gideon, and to his house."

If Gideon had observed the rule enforced by Joshua at Jericho, he would have fared better. If taking no spoil in war were the universal rule, half the wars would never have been waged.

The Midianites " lifted up their heads no more. And the country was in quietness forty years in the days of Gideon," but his success seems to have gone to his head. The poor farmer, who protested that he was the least in his father's house, took unto himself many wives and they bare him seventy sons, but the throne went to Abimilech, the son of a concubine who slew all but one of his seventy half-brothers.

When Gideon died, the Children of Israel turned again to Baalim and made Baal-Beroth their god. Gideon's impression was not as deep or as lasting as the impression made by Joshua. The Israelites not only soon forgot God, but they showed no kindness to Gideon's family in return for " the goodness which he had showed unto Israel."

VI

RUTH: THE DUTIFUL DAUGHTER

RUTH 1: 14-22

THE lesson in the life of Ruth falls under four heads.

First, the beauty of Bible literature: If the word of God were a man-made book, claiming neither inspiration nor divine authority, it would still be the greatest of books. No other publication or compilation approaches it in breadth or depth or height, or simplicity, or clearness, or strength or elegance.

It deals with but two subjects, God and man, and considers man in but two aspects, viz., in his relation to God and in his relation to his fellows; and yet, there is woven into the story of man all that is necessary to life, happiness and service.

The Bible begins with the creation of the world and ends with eternal life. It gives us the most perfect expressions of joy and of sorrow, of exaltation and despair. It draws pen pictures of love, devotion and duty—of hatred, revenge and sin of every kind.

Superlative Illustrations.

Whatever it deals with it leaves nothing to be added.

If it turns the light upon faith, it gives us the superlative illustration of it—" Though he slay me, yet will I trust him."

If it condemns ingratitude, it sounds forth a rebuke

—" But where are the nine? " which has echoed through nineteen hundred years.

When it measures the priceless value of the immortal part of us it weighs all other things in the balance against it and asks, " What shall it profit a man if he shall gain the whole world and lose his own soul? "

It warns against pride " riding for a fall " and exalts repentance rewarded with forgiveness.

In the Psalms we have prayer and praise, thanksgiving and imprecation, agonising suffering and the songs of victory.

One can find in this one book every mood and passion reflected in language of surpassing appropriateness —the blessedness of righteousness in the first, the comfort of trustfulness in the twenty-third, and the courage and confidence that come with faith in nearly every chapter.

In Proverbs we find a store of wisdom, expressed in epigram, that furnishes warning signs for every dangerous point on life's journey from the cradle to the grave.

No young man can go wrong if he will read and obey the words of Solomon. To his negative virtues, strengthened by Proverbs, he can add all affirmative excellence if he will but build his life on the Sermon on the Mount.

The story of Ruth is told in language that would immortalise any author—even more, a reputation could be built on the two verses which contain Ruth's pledge of love and loyalty to her mother-in-law.

Where has love between women been so tenderly expressed? Where has assurance of fidelity found language more fitting?

Second : The beauty and eloquence of the words are less important than the virtue which they embody. The rhetoric is perfect, but the substance is vastly more important than the form.

Ruth's Immortal Words.

Naomi and her husband, Jew and Jewess, were driven by famine from Judah into the land of Moab. Their sons, Mahlon and Chilion, married two heathen women, Orpah and Ruth. As the years went by death entered the home of Naomi and carried away her husband and both of her sons.

The widow thought to solve in a very natural way the problem forced upon her; she would go back to her own people to pass her remaining days and leave her young daughters-in-law to make new alliances among their people. When she communicated her plan to Orpah and Ruth, both protested and expressed a very earnest wish to return with her.

When Naomi, sacrificing her own happiness for what she believed to be the best interests of the daughters-in-law, insisted that they should stay in their own land, Orpah reluctantly consented and kissed her good-bye, " but Ruth clave unto her."

Again Naomi urged her to follow her sister's example. To this Ruth replied in the wonderful plea, " Intreat me not to leave thee, or to return from following after thee." There is dramatic power in each word, " For whither thou goest, I will go; and where thou lodgest, I will lodge." The emphasis increases as her purpose unfolds. " Thy people shall be my people," and then follows the climax that meant so much in the years that followed—" and thy God my God."

The attitude of Orpah and Ruth is a splendid compliment to this mother-in-law.

Many families have been disrupted by antagonism between the members of the family united by ties of blood and those brought into the family by marriage. The mother-in-law joke of today is grievously overdone, although there is friction enough to furnish a basis for it, a fact to which many can bear painful witness.

The confidence and affection existing between Naomi and the wives of her sons would indicate that her mother-love was broad enough to include the wives as well as the sons, and there seemed to be an absence of jealousy on the part of the wives as well as upon the part of the mother.

It was a happy family that might well serve as a model at the present time.

All three of these women deserve praise, but in the darkness of this hour of bereavement Ruth shines out as a star of exceeding brilliancy. Orpah turns back and is lost among her kindred; Naomi lingers a little while upon the stage and then retires into obscurity, while Ruth becomes the central figure in the developments that follow.

Woman's Natural Longing.

" The hour and the man meet," writes the historian— he has written it very often. But " the woman and the hour " also meet—they are meeting more and more —and the same characteristics that make the meeting momentous in the case of men make it momentous also in the case of women.

Third: Ruth sought a husband and found him. Her plans were modest and effective. The heart of Boaz was won by her beauty and by her industry, and it was a generous heart, as proven by the orders that he gave to the reapers when he found Ruth gleaning in the field.

Who shall deny to woman the right to realise the hope that nestles in every normal heart? Marriage is the natural state, a fact conclusively proven by the necessity for it. That without which the race would die must be counted as the normal thing.

Circumstances may suspend the law or consecration to some important task may justify an exception, but marriage is the rule that God has written upon our natures.

Ruth heard the call of the home and responded to it with all her heart, just as men and women have responded before and since her time. The opening of new avenues to women does not close the road to maternity; motherhood must remain the crowning glory of woman, just as man's largest work must continue to be at the fireside.

" The Day of Small Things."

Fourth: When Ruth solved her problem by choosing the companionship of Naomi, identification with Naomi's people and the worship of Naomi's God, she had no idea of the high destiny that that decision ushered in.

Her heart had linked itself to the heart of her husband's mother and she chose to unite herself with the people of her mother-in-law, but she could not look into the future and see how this decision would make her the wife of Boaz—neither did she dream of having as her great grandson the Psalmist, David, and, as a more remote descendant, the mother of Jesus.

" Despise not the day of small things " is an old adage and it is based upon a great truth. Small things

often become the great things. We cannot look very
far into the future—"Lead, kindly Light. . . . One
step enough for me," embodies a very wholesome and
practical philosophy.

Tolstoy says that God has not given us the power to
foresee the results that follow from a single human act,
but that He does give us the light to determine where
and how to take the next step; that is sufficient.

The Russian philosopher goes farther and declares
that most of our failures come from an attempt to
decide whether in this particular case—not as a rule,
but just in this one case—it may not be better to do
wrong than to do right.

We must have " faith in the wisdom of doing right "
—we must do right and leave the consequences with
God.

Importance of Trivial Decisions.

We have seen how Moses, timid and distrusting his
own ability, undertook the task entrusted to him and,
speaking the words that God bade him speak and doing
the things that God told him to do, liberated a people
from bondage—receiving strength for each new step
that he was called upon to take. The decision meant
everything to him and to his people.

We have seen Joseph following his conscience into
the dungeon and, through the dungeon, to a position
next to Pharaoh.

In innumerable cases in Holy Writ and in daily life
we see seemingly trivial decisions become the turning
points in lives and little circumstances shaping destinies.
A multitude of seemingly little things made up the
chain of events that linked Ruth to the throne of Israel.

A famine drove Elimelech from his home into a

heathen land; one of his sons became the husband of Ruth; then the death of husband and sons led Naomi to return. This brought a crisis into the life of her daughter-in-law and she decided to return to her home and Ruth decided to return with her.

Then follows the gleaning in the field, the meeting with Boaz, the marriage, the birth of Obed, and circumstance after circumstance until her blood was coursing through the veins of Israel's greatest king, and later flowed from Calvary.

If any link had been missing the chain would have been broken, but somehow no link is missing when any great character is needed or any great deed is to be done.

Ruth's Faith Can Be Ours.

There is but one Naomi, but one Ruth, and one David; but every human life is like the life of Ruth in miniature—full of decisions, the importance of which no one can understand at the time, but decisions upon which lives turn and by which history is written.

We cannot hope to contribute to literature a sentence so exquisite and so thrilling as that into which Ruth poured the full measure of a noble heart, but we can imitate her in devotion—the brightest jewel in her crown.

She risked all when she made her choice—separation from her sister, her people, and the gods which her people worshipped, but she won a prize of inestimable value.

The same faith can be manifested in every life; for all of us the future holds moments as fateful as that which three deaths combined to bring to Naomi's daughter-in-law.

VII

JOB: THE PATIENT

Job 1-42

JOB is one of the most majestic of the Bible characters. We cannot locate him in any particular century; some commentators insist that he lived before Moses, while others contend that he lived after Solomon. Exactness in chronology is of minor importance since the truths he enunciated are equally applicable to all ages. Dr. G. Campbell Morgan declares the Book of Job to be " in magnificence of argument and beauty of style, one of the grandest in the Divine Library."

The Book of Job begins with a eulogy of Job. He lived in the land of Uz and is described as a man " who was perfect and upright and one that feared God and eschewed evil." He was a fortunate man, the father of seven sons and three daughters, the owner of seven thousand sheep, three thousand camels, five hundred yoke of oxen, five hundred she asses; he had a large household and was " the greatest of all the men of the east." He was a righteous man—so conscientious that when his children feasted the father offered burnt offerings for them, saying, " It *may* be my sons have sinned, and cursed God in their heart."

Then begins the story of Satan's efforts to destroy Job. He is represented as a real being, " going to and fro in the earth " and " walking up and down in it." When the Lord directed his attention to Job, declaring that there was none like him in the earth, Sătan answered, " Doth Job fear God for nought?

" Hast not thou made an hedge about him, and about his house, and about all that he hath on every side? thou hast blessed the work of his hands, and his substance is increased in the land."

There is a very important lesson concealed in Satan's question. He had taken notice of the fact that *righteousness* and *prosperity* are linked together, but he made a mistake (it has often been made since) of reversing cause and effect. Satan thought that Job was good *because* God had blessed him, whereas his blessings were the *result* of his goodness. God has linked our virtue to our happiness and our success to our righteousness. How else could He have constructed a universe upon a moral basis? When the divine law of rewards is allowed to have its way, " the perfect and upright man " is the greatest of all men, whether of the east or the west or of the north or the south.

Satan's Error.

Erroneously supposing that Job was upright because he was hedged about by God's favour, Satan quite naturally thought that misfortune would alienate the good man from the Heavenly Father; he challenged Jehovah to test Job by taking away all that he had— then, said the Evil One, " he will curse thee to thy face."

The Lord's reply was, " Behold all that he hath is in thy power, only upon himself put not forth thine hand." Is it possible that a perfect and an upright man can be tempted and tested—tried in the fire? Yes, examples are needed and only the upright can furnish them. Job's example was a lesson for his day, and it has been a lesson of incalculable value throughout the centuries. Millions upon millions have found new courage in the patience with which he endured suffering and in the faith which was steadfast in spite of all the calamities that befell him.

First: the oxen and the asses were stolen and the servants that kept them were slain; then the sheep were burned and the servants with them; then the camels were stolen and carried away and the servants put to the sword. After all his property had been swept away his children were taken—Satan had done his worst. Many a man, yes, many a woman, has lost faith and turned against God for causes that were trivial compared with the losses that Job suffered. Adversity has been sufficient to bring spiritual insolvency upon some of little faith, and the loss of children has occasionally brought rebellion into hearts that seemed strong in trust. But amid all his misfortunes Job was unshaken. He gave way to grief, but in his sorrow he " fell down upon the ground and worshipped." Then follows the first of his sublime expressions of faith: " Naked came I out of my mother's womb, and naked shall I return thither; the Lord gave and the Lord hath taken away; blessed be the name of the Lord." " In all this Job sinned not, nor charged God foolishly." What could be more beautiful?

When Satan came again the Lord rejoiced in the integrity of Job, and Satan, ignoring the failure of his prediction in regard to Job, shifted his position and asked permission to put Job to a test which he thought more severe than the one the good man had already undergone. " Skin for skin, yea all that man hath will he give for his life," boasted Satan. " but put forth thine hand now, and touch his bone and his flesh, and he will curse thee to thy face."

"And the Lord said unto Satan, Behold, he is in thine hand; but save his life" (2:6).

"So went Satan forth from the presence of the Lord, and smote Job with sore boils from the sole of his foot unto his crown" (2:7).

Job's affliction was so sore, his pain so great, that his wife—even his wife—was in despair and said to him, "Dost thou still retain thine integrity? Curse God and die." Is this one of the few cases where the woman was weaker than the man? Or did her sympathy for him make her anguish deeper than his own? Philosophising is vain; whether Job suffered less in the flesh than she suffered in her mind or whether his heart was more steadfast, he replied to her with a second illustration of perfect trust: "What, shall we receive good at the hand of God and shall we not receive evil?" "In all this did not Job sin with his lips."

His expression of faith found in the thirteenth chapter, verse 15, reaches the climax in strength: "Though he slay me, yet will I trust in him." How it stirs the blood! Job defended his integrity against the accusation of his censorious friends, answering them with courage and spirit, but he bowed before the Almighty and would not bring an indictment against His justice, His wisdom or His love, even in the face of death.

Job Further Tested.

Where in all profane history can be found such an exalted conception of a Supreme Being and so pure and complete a faith?

Then follows a test as severe as the loss of all that he had—as severe as his terrible bodily affliction; he

endured the criticism of his three friends, Eliphaz the
Temanite, Bildad the Shuhite, and Zophar the Naam-
athite.　They came together " to mourn with him and
to comfort him."　Eliphaz has been characterised as a
mystic, Bildad as a traditionalist, and Zophar as a
dogmatist.　But whatever they deserve to be called,
they not only added to the misery of Job, but brought
down upon themselves the condemnation of Jehovah as
recorded in the seventh verse of the last chapter:

" And it was so, that after the Lord had spoken these
words unto Job, the Lord said to Eliphaz the Temanite,
My wrath is kindled against thee, and against thy two
friends: for ye have not spoken of me the thing that is
right, as my servant Job hath."

The three-against-one debate which they carried on
gave to Job an opportunity to embed in the literature of
all time some of the grandest of thoughts expressed in
language that has never been surpassed.

He asked the awful question that has, from the beginning of time, disturbed the thought of the race: " If
a man die, shall he live again? "　His answer indicates
an abiding faith in a future life: " All the days of my
appointed time will I wait, till my change come.　Thou
shalt call and I will answer thee."

His description of man's brief stay upon earth is a
classic: " He cometh forth like a flower, and is cut
down: he fleeth also as a shadow, and continueth not."
His tribute to the grave is one of the most frequently
quoted of his passages: " There the wicked cease from
troubling; and there the weary be at rest.　There the
prisoners rest together; they hear not the voice of the
oppressor.　The small and great are there; and the
servant is free from his master."　And again: " My
days are swifter than a weaver's shuttle."

Job has furnished us with one of the keenest bits of sarcasm ever used. Answering Zophar, he said, " No doubt but ye are the people and wisdom shall die with you."

His knowledge of the stars is displayed in his praise of the Almighty: " Which alone spreadeth out the heavens, and treadeth upon the waves of the sea.

" Which maketh Arcturus, Orion, and Pleiades, and the chambers of the south."

Elihu's Wisdom.

After Eliphaz, Bildad, and Zophar had ceased speaking, silenced by Job's answers, a young man named Elihu, the son of Barachel, came forward and condemned both the three friends and the suffering patriarch. He modestly deferred to those who were older until they were worsted in the discussion. " I am young," he said, " and ye are very old; wherefore I was afraid, and durst not show you my opinion. I said, Days should speak and multitude of years should teach wisdom." Having offered his apology, he grew more bold and added, " But there is a spirit in man; and the inspiration of the Almighty giveth understanding. Great men are not always wise, neither do the aged understand judgment. Therefore I said, Hearken to me; I also will show mine opinion."

He then proceeds to point out the infinite distance between God and man and the sin of vanity and self-righteousness. His argument is a connecting link between the prolonged dispute between Job and his friends and chapter thirty-eight, in which the Lord completes the humiliation of Job and brings him to a knowledge of his sinful assumption of extraordinary wisdom and superior virtue.

Job made no answer to the young man. The Lord brought the dispute to an end with such a display of power that Job was shamed into a confession of his sinfulness. Beginning with a challenging demand: " Who is this that darkeneth counsel by words without knowledge? " the Lord exposed the littleness of man's wisdom and the weakness of man's strength.

" Where wast thou when I laid the foundations of the earth? declare, if thou hast understanding.

" Who hath laid the measures thereof, if thou knowest? or who hath stretched the line upon it?

" Whereupon are the foundations thereof fastened? or who laid the cornerstone thereof:

" When the morning stars sang together, and all the sons of God shouted for joy?

" Who hath divided a water-course for the overflowing waters, or a way for the lightning of thunder;

" To cause it to rain on the earth, where no man is; on the wilderness, wherein there is no man:

" To satisfy the desolate and waste ground; and to cause the bud of the tender herb to spring forth?

" Hath the rain a father? or who hath begotten the drops of dew?

" Out of whose womb came the ice? and the hoary frost of heaven, who hath gendered it?

" The waters are hid as with a stone, and the face of the deep is frozen.

" Canst thou bind the sweet influences of Pleiades, or loose the bands of Orion?

" Canst thou bring forth Mazzaroth in his season? or canst thou guide Arcturus with his sons?

" Knowest thou the ordinances of heaven? canst thou set the dominion thereof in the earth?

" Canst thou lift up thy voice to the clouds, that abundance of waters may cover thee?

" Canst thou send lightnings, that they may go, and say unto thee, Here we are? "

When the Lord concluded with the searching question, " Shall he that contendeth with the Almighty instruct him? He that reproveth God, let him answer it "; Job replied, " Behold, I am vile, what shall I answer thee? "

When the Lord addressed to him a new series of questions, Job answered with a broken and contrite heart, " Wherefore, I abhor myself, and repent in dust and ashes."

When a Mortal Stands in God's Presence.

Here we have a man perfect and upright in comparison with his fellow-men—a man whose integrity had stood the test and whose faith had risen to a height never surpassed; and yet, when he came face to face with God his perfection seemed vile and his self-righteousness a thing to be repented of. His virtues that seemed mountain high as he indignantly repelled the slanders of his accusers vanished in the light of God's wisdom and power and love.

And repentance was rewarded, even back in those far-away years. The forgiveness of sins, made complete for each and all in Christ's death upon the Cross, was foreshadowed in the experiences of Job. " The Lord also accepted Job and the Lord turned the captivity of Job when he prayed for his friends." He was resentful when the three friends criticised him, but when he was humbled by God's answer he prayed for those who had persecuted him. " Also the Lord gave Job twice as much as he had before. . . . So the

Lord blessed the latter end of Job more than his beginning."

We are children of a Father who, having created all things, is able to do as He wills; and He wills to do that which is best for His children. He is even more willing to give than earthly parents. He has so made the world that "all things work together for good to them that love God, to them who are the called according to His purpose."

Job is an example not only in patience but in faith, and his final triumph is an inspiration to those who suffer. "Weeping may endure for a night, but joy cometh in the morning."

VIII

SAMUEL: THE LAST OF THE JUDGES

I SAMUEL 12: 1-5, 20-25

IN Samuel, judge and prophet, we have one of the most beautiful characters in the Old Testament; and in our brief review of his life we shall consider three great lessons that his life holds for twentieth-century men and women everywhere. For Samuel is one of the immortals; his career a shining beacon to all who would walk uprightly and do the will of God.

First: Let us consider the power of a mother's prayer.

Hannah, who was to be the mother of Samuel, was a devout woman, one of the two wives of Elkanah. She longed for a man-child that she might consecrate him to the service of Jehovah, but she was childless and advanced in age.

The other wife, Peninnah, had children and was unkind enough to reproach Hannah, which made the latter's affliction even more bitter.

At the risk of introducing what may seem to some a bit of humour, I venture to call attention to the words used by Hannah's husband in his awkward attempt to comfort her. Noticing that she was weeping, and knowing the cause, he asked: " Why is thy heart grieved? Am I not better to thee than ten sons? "

The best of husbands can hardly hope to entirely take the place of a son. A mother's heart is large enough to love both husband and child, but it is through the child that she most influences the ages, and the suffering through which she passes to win the honour of maternity gives her an inextinguishable title to her offspring.

She invests her life in her children, and where her treasure is, there is her heart also.

Mother and Son.

Divorces between husbands and wives are, unfortunately, more than occasional, but a mother is rarely divorced from her son. He may be heartless, but she forgives; he may desert her, but she hopes for his return—hopes and prays, and her prayers are often answered.

Hannah had a double interest in bringing into the world a son. With a mother's love there was entwined a desire to have one of her own flesh and blood brought up in God's service.

So when she went up with her husband to Shiloh to make the annual sacrifice, she prayed that her heart's wish might be granted and vowed a vow to give her son "unto the Lord all the days of his life" if her prayer was answered; and it was answered.

Mothers' Prayers.

Hannah was the prototype of a multitude of mothers in whose lives religion has been the controlling factor. Finding their greatest joy in the service of their Heavenly Father, they have led their sons to the altar and from their very birth impressed upon them the high calling of the servant of God.

Prayers innumerable have ascended to the throne,

not only for sons, but in behalf of sons. Mothers have felt that they were sufficiently rewarded if their sons realised their hopes, and who will deny the fullness of the reward?

What else can one do that is so valuable as to contribute a human life to the world and then so direct it as to make it a blessing to mankind. How insignificant seems the gorgeous tomb that marks the final resting place of one who has merely absorbed from society—how insignificant, I repeat—in comparison with these monuments of flesh and blood, left by obscure heroines whose graves are forgotten!

There is no influence so lasting as that which passes from one heart to another, running like an electric current through the endless chain of the race.

Serving the Lord Early.

The second lesson I shall draw from Samuel's life is to be found in his early entrance on the Lord's work.

He went as a child into the house of Eli, the priest, who was growing old, and there ministered unto the Lord. One night when he was asleep the Lord called him. Thinking it was Eli's voice, he ran unto the priest and said, " Here am I."

Eli said, " I called not; lie down again."

A second time the voice awakened Samuel and the second time he appeared before Eli, only to be sent back to bed. A third time Samuel was summoned and then Eli, perceiving that it was the Lord's voice that had awakened the child, said:

" Go, lie down: and it shall be, if he call thee, that thou shalt say, Speak, Lord; for thy servant heareth."

When the fourth call came, Samuel answered as he had been advised and the Lord revealed to Samuel the judgment that he had recorded against Eli, and this judgment Samuel made known to the priest when the latter demanded to know what the Lord had communicated to him.

From that day Samuel grew stronger in the Lord's service and became one of the greatest of the prophets of Israel.

A Wicked Excuse.

It is not uncommon for grown people to excuse the sins of youth with the remark that " young men must sow their wild oats." Samuel's life is a conclusive answer to this false philosophy.

There is no reason why any young man should pass through a period of transgression before he settles down to serious and sober work. The experience of the prodigal son is not a necessary introduction to a successful life, neither is the joy of repentance a sufficient recompense for the sorrows of wayward years.

There is an old story of a father who, to impress his son with his recklessness, suggested to him that he drive a nail into a certain post every time he did wrong and pull out a nail every time he did a deserving act.

The nails gradually increased in number as the boy honestly rendered an account of sins committed. Finally, they became so numerous that the boy, through a sense of shame, turned over a new leaf, as they say, and began to withdraw nails as his good deeds exceeded in number his bad ones.

One day he stood before the post from which every nail had been withdrawn, but he was weeping. When his father tried to comfort him by calling attention to the fact that the nails were all gone, the boy replied, " Yes, but the scars are there."

Yes, every sin leaves a scar. The recollection of them haunts the memory and causes distress even when repentance has brought a sense of forgiveness. Some sins run in the blood and curse children before they are born. In thousands of cases the drunkenness and immorality of parents have closed the door of hope on little children before their eyes have opened to the light of day.

Nothing but religion can give one strength to resist the temptations that make the days of youth the critical days in life. Happy is the child who early hears the call of the Father and, hearing, obeys.

Christianity presents the same moral standard to man and to woman; it requires the same temperance and the same chastity in both. No man can, in conscience, require higher ideals in his wife than those that he follows himself—much less can he afford to throw upon a wife the painful duty of warning a child against the example of a father.

An Upright Life.

Third: In Samuel we see the triumph of an upright life.

Our text takes up the career of Samuel when he was about ready to surrender his office of ruler of his people to Saul, their first king. He had held the most exalted position known to his time.

The prophet in Israel was greater than the king; it was his business to admonish and to rebuke the ruler upon his throne, and the great prophets in Israel lived up to this high duty. It was also the prophet's duty to advise the people and in this, too, Samuel was faithful to his trust.

Samuel was an example to all in authority, and that

example was never more needed than now, and never more valuable than in our own beloved land:

"And now, behold, the king walketh before you; and I am old and grayheaded; and, behold, my sons are with you: and I have walked before you from my childhood unto this day.

"Behold, here I am: witness against me before the Lord, and before his anointed: whose ox have I taken? or whose ass have I taken? or whom have I defrauded? whom have I oppressed? or of whose hand have I received any bribe to blind mine eyes therewith? and I will restore it you.

"And they said, Thou hast not defrauded us, nor oppressed us, neither hast thou taken aught of any man's hand.

"And he said unto them, The Lord is witness against you, and his anointed is witness this day, that ye have not found aught in my hand. And they answered, He is witness."

A Glorious Tribute.

He had walked before his people from his youth, conscious of his rectitude. If he had ever defrauded or oppressed any or received a bribe he was ready to restore it before all the people. And the people acquitted him of all wrong.

What a glorious tribute! What pecuniary reward— what profit that comes with power, what pleasure purchased by betrayal of the people can weigh in the balance against the verdict, "Well done, thou good and faithful servant"?

In times of peace we sometimes read of graft on the part of officials. Purchasing agents are required to give bonds, and even bonds do not always restrain the temptations to indirect larceny. Every device that cunning can employ is used to extract money from the public treasury. The corruption of legislators became so notorious that the method of electing United States Senators was changed in order to protect our highest legislative body from scandals of this kind. And even direct election has not entirely eliminated bribery.

But, more shocking still, even the patriotic sentiment aroused by war could not restrain some of those entrusted by the government with large undertakings. The people, bleeding at the battle's front and burdened by such taxes as they had never borne before, were plundered by men to whom the people looked for unselfish service. This was true in this country and in other countries as well—in Christian countries, too.

Four Great Needs.

The great need of the world today—not of the United States alone, but of the whole world—is a return to a real belief in a real God.

We need more consecrated mothers like Hannah, to bear children for the Lord's work, and to train them for their tasks.

And we need more women, too, who will see in life a purpose higher than mere fleeting pleasure—women who, counting themselves part of God's plan, will seek to know the Father's will that they may be obedient to it.

We need more men like Samuel to begin the service of God in youth and continue to walk uprightly all their days.

We also need more public officials in city, state, and nation who, guided by conscience, will not abuse their privileges or embezzle power.

There is a motto that ought to be written over the door of every public building and engraven on the heart of everyone who serves the people. It is this:

"A good name is rather to be chosen than great riches, and loving favour rather than silver and gold."

IX

DAVID: THE SHEPHERD KING

I Samuel 16: 1-13

IN this study we consider one of the outstanding
figures in Hebrew history—David, who was more
than a king: he was a warrior and a poet. Characteristics seldom found together were not only combined in him, but were developed to a very high degree.

" Surely goodness and mercy shall follow me all the
days of my life "—this passage from the Twenty-third
Psalm gives expression to a spirit of gratitude that
finds in David's utterances more frequent, more emphatic and more beautiful forms of expression than
can be found in the words of any other mortal known
to history.

Our text records the selection and anointing of
David by the prophet Samuel. The first verse contains
a rebuke to Samuel, administered by the Lord when the
prophet hesitated about making known to the king the
Lord's decree. Samuel feared Saul, but obeyed the
command of God when he received directions as to the
selection of Saul's successor.

Jesse, the son of Obed, and grandson of Ruth, was
to have the honour of having a son upon the throne of
Israel. Then follows an intensely interesting account
of the selection of David.

Jesse made seven of his sons to pass before Samuel.
The first was Eliab, the eldest. He was evidently a
man of striking appearance and Samuel was pleased

with him, but the Lord discarded him, saying to Samuel:

"Look not on his countenance, or on the height of his stature; because I have refused him: for the Lord seeth not as man seeth; for man looketh on the outward appearance, but the Lord looketh on the heart."

Here we find an important truth, as we find others scattered through the Old and New Testament.

Man is prone to look on the outward appearance and, therefore, is being constantly deceived in men. "The Lord looketh on the heart," the seat of purpose and of virtue. "Out of the heart are the issues of life"; "As a man thinketh in his heart, so is he."

Jesse then called six other sons, but none of them proved to be the chosen one. Then Samuel said unto Jesse: "Are here all thy children?"

Jesse answered that the youngest son was keeping sheep. "Send and fetch him," commanded Samuel, "for we will not sit down, until he come hither."

First Mention of David.

The next verse of the text introduces David to the world:

"Now he was ruddy, and withal of a beautiful countenance, and goodly to look to, and the Lord said, Arise, anoint him; for this is he.

"Then Samuel took the horn of oil, and anointed him in the midst of his brethren: and the Spirit of the Lord came upon David from that day forward."

The first test of David came when Saul was at war with the Philistines.

The three eldest sons of Jesse were in the king's army and David was sent to carry food to his brothers.

He arrived just in time to see Goliath, the giant, challenging any Israelite to meet him in single combat. He had come forward each day for forty days with his insolent boast and no Israelite dared accept—and it is not strange that they were afraid when it is remembered that Goliath was ten feet in height, and clad in complete armour.

David's Reliance.

The rest of the Israelites relied upon their own strength and, of course, that was not sufficient for this emergency. But David had not relied upon his own strength since "the Spirit of the Lord came mightily" upon him, as the Revised Version has it. His strength was in the Lord and he was not afraid. He at once stepped forward and offered to accept the challenge as a representative for his people.

His brothers, quite naturally, attempted to dissuade him. If they, warriors, were not equal to the task, how foolish for a lad to match his strength against the giant. But David had the insistence that all have who are conscious that they are carrying out the will of God, and that insistence finally overcame the fears and the protests of the disheartened Israelites.

When he obtained permission to meet Goliath, Saul offered him his armour—in fact, clothed him in his armour from head to foot, but David declined, saying that he had not proved it. Then, taking his shepherd's sling and five smooth pebbles from the brook, he went forth to what seemed the most unequal combat recorded in history.

But the first pebble was enough; the giant had heedlessly exposed his forehead, and the pebble sank into the giant's head. David ran forward and, seizing the

giant's own great sword, cut off his head. The Israelites, their courage renewed by David's victory, rushed
forward and the Philistines were routed. David was
acclaimed a hero and the nation's saviour. From that
day forth he had the love of the people and the envy
of the king.

Preparing for God's Work.

Let us pause a moment to draw a moral from this
incident in David's life.

Whenever God has a work to do, He has some-
body prepared for it—the kind of preparation needed
for the work. But the agent of the Lord does not
always know—he seldom knows—the work for which
he is preparing. When this shepherd boy was practicing with his sling, he little thought that the skill which
he was acquiring would be the defense of his people.

Whether his preparation was a result of Divine suggestion or an indication of a desire for thoroughness,
matters not; the disposition to do thoroughly anything
undertaken may have been itself the result of a thought
implanted in his heart by the Almighty and for a purpose. At any rate, he had the skill when the opportunity came to use it, and he so used it as to win favour
at once.

Success may be defined as the conjunction of opportunity and the preparedness to meet it. Those who
prepare well along some line of work are quite sure to
have an opportunity to use their preparation, but opportunities are of no value to those who either do not see
them or, seeing them, are not prepared to take advantage of them.

The second period of David's life was spent in exile,
fleeing from the wrath of Saul. It was a period of

preparation for the work that awaited him and brought out two prominent characteristics:

First: Forbearance. Saul sought to put him to death, but the Lord was with David and led him out of every ambush. Twice David had Saul within his power and twice he spared the life of the king who was eagerly plotting his destruction. Such a forgiving spirit is rare in one whose life is in peril.

Second: An extraordinary affection grew up between him and Saul's son, Jonathan. It stands out as one of the great friendships in history. The Pythian fraternity is built upon the friendship of two Greeks, Damon and Pythias, but the friendship between David and Jonathan is superior in many ways.

Jonathan was the son of the king who sought the life of David and he knew that David had been anointed as the successor of his father; yet he protected this rival aspirant to the throne and he did it at the risk of his own life.

Damon offered himself as a hostage for Pythias—a supreme test of his love—but his confidence in the honour of Pythias would not allow him to feel that he was taking any risk. Jonathan, on the other hand, had no assurance that he could conceal from his father his devotion to one whom his father regarded as an enemy to the kingdom.

David's Grievous Sin.

While David's love for Jonathan did not add as much to his own dangers as Jonathan's love for David endangered him, David was just as willing to assume all of the risks involved. When the Philistines slew Jonathan and an Amalekite came to David with Saul's crown and a bracelet, taken from the king's arm, and reported that he had, at the king's request, dispatched the latter when an attempt at suicide had failed, David caused the Amalekite to be put to death, saying, " How wast thou not afraid to stretch forth thine hand to destroy the Lord's anointed ? "

The death of Saul and Jonathan, sad to David in spite of the fact that it established him upon the throne, called forth one of the greatest of David's psalms; it contained a tribute to Saul—" How are the mighty fallen "; and a tribute to Jonathan—" Thy love to me was wonderful, passing the love of women."

A word as to David's grievous sin.

In surrendering to passion he was guilty of the greatest of iniquities, no more excusable in that age than now, but his repentance was as sincere as his guilt was deep. The consciousness of the enormity of his sin stirred his very soul and broadened the language in which he pleads against wrongdoing and defends the justice of the decree of the Almighty.

He did the only thing that a sinner can do by way of atonement—he used his sorrow to warn others against forbidden paths.

" Sweet Singer of Israel."

As king, he protected his people from attack and strengthened their position as a nation; he was a stalwart teacher of righteousness and exerted a lasting influence upon the thought of the Children of Israel. He was an heroic personality and as virile spiritually as he was intellectually and politically.

But it is as " the sweet singer of Israel " that he has touched the hearts of the generations that succeeded him. His thoughts were lofty and his language as lofty as his thought. He had a wonderful vision of human

life and the heights that it may reach under divine
direction:

" Thou hast made him a little lower than the angels,
and hast crowned him with glory and honour. Thou
madest him to have dominion over the works of thy
hands: thou hast put all things under his feet."

Having thus given man superlative praise, he shows
how little man is in comparison with the Maker of all
things: " Man is like to vanity: his days are as a
shadow that passeth away."

He exalted God and magnified His name. He drew
illustrations from all nature and turned all things
to the praise of his Maker. " The heavens declare
the glory of God; and the firmament sheweth his
handiwork."

He inspired courage by explaining its source: " The
Lord is the strength of my life; of whom shall I be
afraid? "

David has given to those about to die the most com-
forting words to be found in the Old Testament: " The
Lord is my shepherd; I shall not want.

" He maketh me to lie down in green pastures; he
leadeth me beside the still waters.

" He restoreth my soul; he leadeth me in the paths
of righteousness for his name's sake.

" Yea, though I walk through the valley of the
shadow of death, I will fear no evil; for thou art with
me; thy rod and thy staff they comfort me."

Only in the New Testament do we find language
more assuring:

" I go to prepare a place for you. And if I go and
prepare a place for you, I will come again, and receive
you unto myself; that where I am, there ye may be
also."

X

SOLOMON: THE WISE

SOLOMON, the subject of this chapter, occupies a unique place among the heroes of the Old Testament. He was a king, a position held by but few of the great men of Israel, and, what was no less peculiar, he was the son of a king. His father, the Shepherd King and Psalmist of his people, reared him for the throne and lavished upon him his love and tender care. He was the child of a favourite wife and manifested extraordinary ability at an early age. *The Song of Solomon* is supposed to have been written before he ascended the throne.

The name, Solomon, means "Peaceable." His reign began with an era of peace. His assumption of kingly power was marked by rare humility; his petition for wisdom set the mark for officials of all the ages since.

A Father's Prayer for His Son.

The seventy-second Psalm contains David's prayer for his son, and it is a noble plea. David set him on a high pedestal and prescribed for him a sacred task: "He shall judge the poor of the people, he shall save the children of the needy." And again: "He shall deliver the needy when he crieth; the poor also, and him that hath no helper." And still again: "His name shall endure forever; his name shall be continued as

78

long as the sun; and men shall be blessed in him: all nations shall call him blessed."

The Lord appeared unto Solomon in a dream and said, " Ask what I shall give thee. And Solomon said, Thou hast shewed unto thy servant David my father great mercy, according as he walked before thee in truth, and in righteousness, and in uprightness of heart with thee; and thou hast kept for him this great kindness, that thou hast given him a son to sit on his throne, as it is this day.

" And now, O Lord my God, thou hast made thy servant king instead of David my father: and I am but a little child: I know not how to go out or come in. . . . Give therefore thy servant an understanding heart to judge thy people, that I may discern between good and bad: for who is able to judge this thy so great a people? And the speech pleased the Lord, that Solomon had asked this thing.

" And God said unto him, Because thou hast asked this thing, and hast not asked for thyself long life; neither hast asked riches for thyself, nor hast asked the life of thine enemies; but has asked for thyself understanding to discern judgment: Behold, I have done according to thy words; lo, I have given thee a wise and an understanding heart; so that there was none like thee before thee, neither after thee shall any arise like unto thee."

The verses quoted present three thoughts:

First: Solomon asked for the greatest blessing that could come to one in authority—" an understanding heart to judge thy people that I might discern between good and bad." That, today, is the great need of officialdom throughout the world. There are brains enough and to spare; no one is likely to reach a high

official position who is deficient in intelligence, but
multitudes have swayed the sceptre who not only were
unable to discern between right and wrong, but who
were not concerned to know what was right. No matter what the form of government, the highest requirement for officials is the same for all, a heart that is in
sympathy with the people—an understanding heart that
can judge the people with justice and discern between
good and evil.

Second: Solomon received that for which he asked.
God was pleased with the request that he made and
promised him wisdom such as no one had had before
him and—mark the words—would be possessed by no
one after him. Here is a chance to test the veracity of
the Scriptures. Some deny that God ever spake to
man. We have in these verses a record of what God
said. The statement attributed to the Almighty is
either true or false, and it can be *tested* and thus proven
or disproven. Where *before* Solomon can such a compilation of wisdom be found, and where *since?* Let the
sceptic consider the age in which Solomon lived and
the environment that surrounded him. Where, except
from above, could he have found the truths which he
announced, the advice which he gave on every question
that arises in our daily lives?

Third: God not only gave him the wonderful gift
for which he asked, but added also the things which
men are prone to crave. Because he asked not for long
life or for riches or for the life of his enemies, God
bestowed upon him *riches* and *honour* and, upon *condition,* long life also. The condition was: "If thou
wilt walk in my ways, to keep my statutes and my commandments." And does not God do the same today?
Riches and honour are the recompense to one who has

an understanding heart and is able to discern between right and wrong, and length of days are the reward given today, as well as in olden times, to those who walk in God's ways and keep His commandments.

The Builder of the Temple of Jehovah.

To Solomon, a man of peace, fell the task for which David, the man of war, was not fitted, namely, the task of building a temple for the Lord. The work was entrusted to two Hirams—Hiram king of Tyre, who furnished the cedar and the fir, and Hiram of Naphtali, who was a worker in brass. It was a wonderful edifice, a monument to the devotion of Solomon and his people and a monument, also, to the skill of the workmen.

When the temple was completed, the Lord appeared unto Solomon a second time as He had appeared unto him at Gibeon. Here again the covenant between the Lord and Solomon contained a condition: If Solomon would walk before God as David his father had walked, in integrity of heart and in uprightness; if he would keep the statutes and judgments of the Almighty, then, said the Lord, " I will establish the throne of thy kingdom upon Israel forever." But—then follows the warning (I quote from " The Holy Scriptures, According to the Masaretic Text, A New Translation," issued by the Jewish Publication Society of America, Philadelphia)—" If ye shall turn away from following me, ye or your children, and not keep my commandments and my statutes which I have set before you, but shall go and serve other gods and worship them, then will I cut off Israel out of the land which I have given them; and this house which I have hallowed for my name, will I cast out of my sight; and Israel shall be a proverb and a by-word among all people."

Let those who scoff at prophecy visit Jerusalem today and see the ruins of this temple; they will find at " The Wailing Place " of those who mourn the overthrow of Solomon's temple the most pathetic scene that one looks upon in a trip around the world.

The Great Book of Wisdom.

But let us consider the Book of Proverbs, Solomon's chief contribution to the literature of the world. If I may be pardoned a personal reference, my father, as devout a man as ever lived, early impressed upon my youthful mind and heart the value of Solomon's advice. He would call me in from work a little before noon to read and comment on a chapter in Proverbs. I am afraid that I did not always appreciate the priceless wisdom of the book from which he read. But when he died, just after I reached my twentieth year, I recalled his interest in the words of Solomon and read Proverbs through once a month for a year—an easy task, since there are just thirty-one chapters in the book. I so fully share in the high estimate that he placed upon Proverbs that I have lost no opportunity to commend them to young men.

The proverb, like the epigram, is valuable because it says a great deal in a few words. It puts truth in its most effective form because it can be easily remembered.

Note Solomon's enumeration of the seven things that are an abomination to the Lord; they read as if they were written this very day:

" A proud look, a lying tongue, and hands that shed innocent blood; An heart that deviseth wicked imaginations, feet that be swift in running to mischief, a false witness that speaketh lies, and he that soweth discord among brethren."

He is specific in advice and warns against all the temptations which man has to meet. He is especially emphatic in his denunciation of immorality:

" For the lips of a strange woman drop as an honeycomb, and her mouth is smoother than oil:

" But her end is bitter as wormwood, sharp as a two-edged sword.

" Her feet go down to death; her steps take hold on hell " (5:3-5).

And this is the counsel he gives to those who are tempted to drink:

" Who hath woe? who hath sorrow? who hath contentions? who hath babbling? who hath wounds without cause? who hath redness of eyes?

" They that tarry long at the wine; they that go to seek mixed wine.

" Look not thou upon the wine when it is red, when it giveth his colour in the cup, when it moveth itself aright.

" At the last it biteth like a serpent, and stingeth like an adder " (Prov. 23:29-32).

He commends industry:

" Seest thou a man diligent in his business? he shall stand before kings; he shall not stand before mean men " (Prov. 22:29).

" Go to the ant, thou sluggard; consider her ways, and be wise " (6:6).

Behold the estimate he places upon a good name:

" A good name is rather to be chosen than great riches, and loving favour rather than silver and gold " (22:1).

And consider the tribute he pays to the upright life:

" The path of the just is as the shining light, that shineth more and more unto the perfect day " (4: 18).

Chapter III is bursting out with verbal riches:

" Let not mercy and truth forsake thee: bind them about thy neck; write them upon the table of thine heart."

" Trust in the Lord with all thine heart; and lean not unto thine own understanding.

" In all thy ways acknowledge him, and he shall direct thy paths."

" Honour the Lord with thy substance, and with the firstfruits of all thine increase:

" So shall thy barns be filled with plenty, and thy presses shall burst out with new wine.

" My son, despise not the chastening of the Lord; neither be weary of his correction:

" For whom the Lord loveth he correcteth; even as a father the son in whom he delighteth " (3: 9-12).

There is nothing finer than his tribute to wisdom (3: 13-17):

" Happy is the man that findeth wisdom, and the man that getteth understanding.

" For the merchandise of it is better than the merchandise of silver, and the gain thereof than fine gold.

" She is more precious than rubies: and all the things thou canst desire are not to be compared unto her.

" Length of days is in her right hand; and in her left hand riches and honour.

" Her ways are ways of pleasantness, and all her paths are peace."

In a few words he enforces one of the most important lessons of life:

" A man's heart deviseth his way; but the Lord directeth his steps " (16:9). Those who trust in God find that His leadings are safer than man's plans.

Here are some sentences selected at random:

" Withhold not good from them to whom it is due, when it is in the power of thine hand to do it " (3:27).

" Strive not with a man without cause, if he have done thee no harm.

" The wise shall inherit glory; but shame shall be the promotion of fools " (3:35).

" The liberal soul shall be made fat, and he that watereth shall be watered also himself " (11:25).

" Weary not thyself to be rich . . . for riches certainly make themselves wings, like an eagle that flieth toward heaven " (23:4, 5).

" My son, hear the instruction of thy father, and forsake not the law of thy mother " (6:20).

" Children's children are the crown of old men; and the glory of children are their father's " (17:6).

" The fear of the Lord is the beginning of knowledge " (1:7).

" Remove far from me vanity and lies: give me neither poverty nor riches: feed me with food convenient for me:

" Lest I be full, and deny thee, and say, Who is the Lord? or lest I be poor, and stead, and take the name of my God in vain " (30:8, 9).

But the selection of extracts is nowhere less satisfactory, because every verse is good. In every perplexity of life one can turn to Proverbs and find comfort and wholesome advice. The last chapter brings together a series of tributes to woman. The aid that a wife can give to her husband is recorded in the twenty-third verse:

" Her husband is known in the gates, when he sitteth among the elders of the land."

Verses one and thirteen of the last chapter of Ecclesiastes give a summary of his philosophy of life:

" Remember now thy Creator in the days of thy youth, while the evil days come not, nor the years draw nigh, when thou shalt say, I have no pleasure in them:

" Let us hear the conclusion of the whole matter: Fear God, and keep his commandments; for this is the whole duty of man.

True Wisdom Comes Only from God.

How disappointing that one who could give such invaluable aid to all generations should, at the end of life, have fallen from his high position. Notwithstanding his own repeated warnings against the ravages of lust, Solomon " loved many strange women, together with the daughter of Pharaoh, women of the Moabites, Ammonites, Edomites, Zidonians and Hittites "—nations against which Israel had been specifically warned. " It came to pass when Solomon was old that his wives turned away his heart after other gods." He worshipped the idols of the heathen and sacrificed unto the gods that his wives worshipped. The punishment promised by the Almighty was visited upon him.

Is not the apostasy of Solomon proof that his words came not *from* him but *through* him? If he had originated such lofty sentiments and himself fashioned such treasures of wisdom for the edification of mankind, it is hardly conceivable that he could have fallen so far below the standard which he himself set up. He was merely the conduit through which heavenly wisdom flowed down from God to man. While he was under the influence of the divine Spirit, he played an heroic part; when left to himself, he proved to be of the earth, earthy. When he walked with God, his head was among the stars; when he walked alone, he was a pigmy, sunken in sensuality, and a worshipper of false gods.

XI

REHOBOAM: THE AUTOCRAT

I KINGS 12:12-20

NOWHERE except in the Bible do we find portrayed so vividly and so abundantly the just retributions that follow wrong doing; nowhere are the rewards of righteousness shown to be more swift and more sure.

Consider Rehoboam, the only son of Solomon. We wonder how one so wise could have a son so foolish—so far as known the sole contribution which he and a thousand wives and concubines made to the perpetuation of the race.

Rehoboam had all the advantages that a youth of his day could have. His father's reign was conspicuous because of its prosperity; wealth poured in upon his kingdom, and the heir-apparent had everything that the worldly-wise think necessary for a favourable environment. But the son taught the lesson so frequently repeated before and since, that neither a great family name, nor learning, nor wealth can insure wisdom.

When Solomon entered upon his reign he prayed, " Give therefore thy servant an understanding heart to judge thy people, that I may discern between good and bad." But nothing was farther from the son's heart than the father's prayer. He came to the throne as his father's successor without a protest, and by one act of folly lost ten of the twelve tribes over which his father ruled.

His first error was to ignore good advice. We read that Rehoboam " consulted with the old men, that stood before Solomon his father while yet he lived, and said, How do ye advise that I may answer this people? "

Jeroboam, who represented the ten tribes of the children of Israel, had presented a petition, saying, " Thy father made our yoke grievous: now therefore make thou the grievous service of thy father, and his heavy yoke which he put upon us, lighter, and we will serve thee."

Refusing Good Counsel.

Whether the yoke was really grievous or whether their complaint was without just grounds is not the material question. The people made complaint and the old men, whom Rehoboam consulted first, advised Rehoboam, saying: " If thou wilt be a servant unto this people this day, and wilt serve them, and answer them, and speak good words to them, then they will be thy servants for ever."

This was sound counsel. The king was advised to serve the people and to speak good words to them upon the assurance that the people would then be his servants.

But such advice did not please the young king. He forsook the counsel of the old men and " consulted with the young men that were grown up with him," and they, influenced possibly by the impetuous spirit of youth, but more likely by a desire to please Rehoboam, gave him advice just the opposite of that given by the old men.

They not only advised him to refuse the people's petition, but they suggested insolent words which could not fail to provoke resentment, if not rebellion.

Instead of promising relief, or even expressing a willingness to investigate the cause of complaint, they advised Rehoboam to threaten heavier burdens. "My little finger shall be thicker than my father's loins" was the illustration which was used to measure the increase that he would impose upon them. Instead of inquiring whether his father's yoke was burdensome, he was told to admit—possibly without justification— that his father's yoke was heavy and say that he would add to it.

This was the advice of the young men, and to make his defiance of the people more contemptuous the young men suggested another simile: "My father hath chastised you with whips, but I will chastise you with scorpions."

How these young men advisers must have giggled and winked at each other as they urged the young king to impudence. Wit is often more alluring than common sense; with some smartness counts more than simple truth.

Rehoboam was easily led when the appeal was made to his pride and self-importance. He doubtless chuckled at the brilliancy of the retort suggested to him and nodded his head as if to say, "We will nip this familiarity in the bud; we'll teach these people not to bother a king with protests and entreaties. Any encouragement would lead to further demands."

The Old Story of Autocracy.

It is the old story of autocracy. The methods of arbitrary government are not new; they are the natural outcroppings when power is not controlled by love.

Pharaoh exercised them when he compelled the children of Israel to make bricks without straw as a punishment. When they asked for time to sacrifice to their God, Pharaoh replied that it was because they were idle that they asked for time to sacrifice, and he commanded " Let there more work be laid upon the men." And the emancipation of the children of Israel followed.

It was in the same spirit that Rehoboam, unmindful of the lessons of the past, dealt with his people, so that the ten tribes of Israel revolted and made Jeroboam their king; and it is interesting to note that Bismarck, in his story of his own life, criticises the King of Prussia's military commander for not being more harsh in dealing with an uprising in 1848.

" On Nov. 10," he says, " Wrangel, having marched in at the head of his troops, negotiated with the civil guard and persuaded them to withdraw voluntarily. I considered that a political mistake. If there had only been the slightest skirmish, Berlin would have been captured, not by capitulation, but by force, and then the political position of the government would have been quite different."

The Moral.

The moral that we draw from this lesson comes at a very appropriate time. The spirit of Pharaoh and Rehoboam has too often been the spirit of the world— not only the spirit of those in control of governments, but the spirit of those who have dominated in all walks of life.

One cannot travel through the lands where so-called inferior people are held as subjects by a superior force without hearing echoes of this autocratic philosophy. " The people will not appreciate any favours shown them." " They will construe kindness as weakness."

" They must be controlled by fear." Peace by terrorism has been a costly fallacy from which the world is now turning.

Rehoboam gives us the antithesis of the spirit of brotherhood, and his failure can be cited today in support of the wisdom of the opposite policy—the brotherhood which Christ taught. " Thou shalt love thy neighbour as thyself " is the remedy—the only remedy —for all the ills which afflict society, whether they come from misgovernment or from friction between different elements of society.

As war, like a boil, indicates poison in the blood, so the domestic boils that appear on the body politic indicate a poison that must be eradicated. Christ is the Great Physician; He purifies the blood and brings to individual, to community, to state, to nation, and to the world that peace for which all hearts yearn.

XII

ASA: THE MONARCH WHO RELIED ON GOD

II CHRONICLES 14:1-12

R EHOBOAM reigned seventeen years, his son Abijah three years, and during those twenty years idolatry was rife throughout Judah. Then there came a day when Abijah slept with his fathers, and Asa, his son, reigned in his stead.

" And Asa did that which was good and right in the eyes of the Lord his God."

He destroyed idolatry. " He took away the altars of the strange gods, and the high places, and brake down the images." And he " commanded Judah to seek the Lord God of their fathers, and to do the law and the commandment."

An Unusual Man.

Asa was an unusual man. He was not only better than his father, but he seems to have had no aid from the woman side of the house. His grandmother was a daughter of Absalom, and an evil woman.

As a rule young men are advised to imitate the virtues of their fathers, and the rule that a man takes his virtues from his mother is still more common. The moral standards of women are usually higher than the moral standards of men—that is why those who profited by vice were unanimously opposed to woman suffrage. They feared her conscience and her home instincts.

93

There are, of course, numerous illustrations of weak husbands being led into error by wicked wives, but much more frequently noble women have rescued, restored and strengthened men. Lady Macbeth is an outstanding figure in drama because she was more resolute in evil-doing than her husband. In the Bible, Jezebel stands for a relatively small class of women. She was a stronger personality than Ahab, and threw her strength on the side of the worship of idols.

There is another character that represents not bold wickedness but weakness of faith, as compared with her husband. Job's wife did not have the patience that her husband displayed. She gave up hope and advised him to " curse God and die." She did not have Job's philosophy, " Shall we receive good at the hands of God, and shall we not receive evil? " or the wonderful faith that led Job to exclaim, " Though he slay me, yet will I trust in him."

But we know people largely by comparison, and it is hardly fair to compare any one with Job. His wife's faith might have been superior to that of most husbands.

The Second Commandment.

Asa's father reigned but a short time, during which he won a notable victory over Jeroboam, first king of the ten revolting tribes of Israel. But he was a weak man and, according to the commentators, permitted idolatry and allowed both himself and his people to commit heathen abominations.

In the Second Commandment we are told that God visits the iniquities of the fathers upon the children to the third and fourth generations of them that hate Him, and shows mercy unto thousands of them that love Him and keep His commandments. Some have questioned the justice of God because He visits the iniquities of the fathers upon the children.

It is not necessary that we shall understand God's laws in order to respect them. The citizen is required to obey the law of the land, even though he opposed its enactment, and that, too, whether it is the proclamation of a king or the decree of a people's government. In human government obedience does not depend upon love for the law or even an understanding of it. If this is true of a man-made law, it is much more true of the laws made by an infinite God for the government of finite people.

It may not be out of place, however, to suggest that the law of heredity acts as a powerful restraint in hours of temptation. A man would more frequently yield to sin if the entire penalty would fall upon himself; he is stronger to withstand temptation when he knows that his act may curse his children and his children's children.

And then there is the other side of the proposition. God shows mercy unto thousands that love Him and keep His commandments. The mercy of God, as well as His punishments, are a matter of inheritance. Man is constrained to an obedience which not only saves himself and those of his blood from the wrath of God, but assures him and them the joy of God's presence and the smile of His approval.

Breaking With the Past.

Asa did that which was good and right in the eyes of the Lord his God. Noble son! He broke with the past, rose above the evil environment of his youth and put his trust in God.

A lesson for every young man who begins life with the handicap of an unfavourable environment. While the majority of such drift with the current and suffer shipwreck, there are enough splendid illustrations of individual strength to make it certain that none need fail. Society will encourage every boy and every girl who is willing to do as Asa did, and the Church should be the first to offer its hand.

Walter Malone preaches the true gospel of Jesus and His Church when he says, " No shamefaced outcast ever sank so deep but he can rise and be again a man." If there is hope for the vilest sinner how much more for the son or daughter of one who has sinned?

But one who would start right must do as Asa did. He took away the foreign altars and the high places and brake down the pillars. As king he was responsible for the form of worship of his people, and he proceeded to do his duty. He rid the land of the altars that had been erected to heathen gods and abolished all the insignia of idol worship.

So with one who sets out upon a new life; he cannot compromise with the things that pertain to the world; his affections cannot cling to the sins of the world. His heart must hate the things that it once loved and love the things that it once hated.

An Example for Those in Authority.

Asa gave evidence of a new birth by the thoroughness with which he destroyed the implements employed in idol worship. He commanded Judah to seek the God of their fathers and to do His law and the commandments.

It was a great thing for a private citizen to turn from sin unto righteousness; it was much greater for a ruler to lead a people in the worship of God. And as today, while every soul is of equal value in the sight of God, and every heart can be made a fit temple for the indwelling of God's Spirit, it is more important that men in authority shall have singleness of purpose and be sensible of responsibility. The blessing reaches its maximum when the rulers of a free people worship Jehovah.

They have a duty to perform today, for altars have been raised to mammon in the market-place and many have turned from the worship of the Heavenly Father to the worship of gold. The nation needs today the recognition of God at Washington and at the state capitals. All the great problems with which the world has to deal are due to a failure to obey God.

Without a worship of God there can be no respect for God's law of rewards. It is a disregard of God's law of rewards that has brought upon our nation its greatest burdens and threatens it with the greatest calamities. According to God's law, each human being is entitled to draw from the common store in proportion to his industry and intelligence. In other words, a man is not entitled to more than he earns, and he cannot earn more than a fair compensation for the service that he renders. When a few are permitted to draw more than they earn the total sum is so reduced that that which remains is not sufficient to give a just compensation to the remainder.

" For We Rest on Thee."

The God-fearing statesmen of the world have a work to do in the bringing of peace. The time is ripe for the emancipation of the people from war. The fullness of time had not come when Asa improved the ten quiet years of his reign to fortify the cities of Judah against the enemies round about. War was then the only method of settling disputes. The land hunger that has caused so many wars in the centuries since Asa's day was even then the cause of strife.

The devil's burden has become too heavy for the nations; they must turn from his sophistries and false philosophies to One whose yoke is easy and whose burden is light. When the Arms Conference met at Washington last fall it was opened with prayer. An appeal was made to the God of our fathers, and every step taken was in the direction of obedience to God's law and His commandments.

Asa relied upon God. "Help us, O Lord our God; for we rest on thee, and in thy name we go against this multitude!" he cried when the great host of the Ethiopians was set in battle array against him.

His example ought to be valuable now to private citizens and to public officials alike. He followed the only path that is open to those who seek to make the most of life for themselves and to make the world a blessed dwelling-place for the children of men.

"Help us, O Lord our God, for we rest on thee."

XIII

ELIJAH: THE MESSENGER OF JEHOVAH

I Kings 17: 1-16

ELIJAH, the Tishbite, one of the greatest of the characters of the Old Testament, appears upon the scene unannounced. We have no information as to his early life. His family history is not known, neither is any light thrown upon his training for his work. We read simply, that he " was of the inhabitants of Gilead."

Like a clap of thunder out of a clear sky—or, since he is sometimes called " the prophet of fire," it might be more appropriate to say like a flash of lightning—he stands before the wicked king Ahab and warns him of a coming drought as punishment for Israel's sin of idol worship.

A word about the king. He was eighth in the succession of the house of Israel, a man of considerable strength, wedded to a wife who was stronger than himself.

Possibly, expediency may have had some part in his selection of her as his wife. The children of Israel were surrounded by the worshippers of Baal and the father of Jezebel stood high among the worshippers of that heathen god. As Ahab's wife, she proceeded to introduce the worship of her people's god among the children of Israel, and the sins of Ahab are largely charged to her account.

The story of our talk is a brief one. One verse tells

of Elijah's appearance before Ahab and the warning of punishment that he uttered; the next verse tells of his being sent to the brook Cherith, " which is before Jordan," to be fed by the ravens. Then follows one of the most familiar and oft-quoted passages in the Bible: " And the ravens brought him bread and flesh in the morning, and bread and flesh in the evening; and he drank of the brook."

Can God Perform a Miracle?

" Fed by the ravens " has come to be a popular description of help from an unexpected source, and literature teems with illustrations that are almost as conclusive proof of providential care as that presented by this incident in the life of Elijah. Those who deny the miraculous have devoted a great deal of attention to this account of nourishment furnished by the fowls of the air. Some try to twist the language so as to have Elijah fed by Arabs, but it is a waste of time and energy unless one rejects the miracle entirely.

We may as well consider the miracle now as later, because it reappears continually in both the Old and New Testaments.

Is there such a thing as a miracle? To those who accept the Bible as it was written and construe it according to the rules which they apply to everyday life, the miracle presents no difficulty.

Can God perform a miracle? Yes, a God who can make a world can do anything He wants to with it.

To deny that God can perform a miracle is to deny that God is God. A God who can make a man and provide ordinary food for him can also provide extraordinary food. A God who can make a raven can direct it in its flight. If the power exists, means can easily be found. The use of unusual means raises no doubts.

But the second question is the one that has given most trouble. Would God *want* to perform a miracle?

To answer that in the negative, one must assume a larger knowledge of God than any one has yet been able to claim. Modesty, if nothing else, would keep a finite mind from assuming thorough acquaintance with all the purposes, plans, and methods of Infinite Intelligence.

When we remember that we do not know the mystery of our own lives, cannot understand the mystery of love that makes life worth living, and cannot solve the mystery wrapped up in everything that we eat and involved in everything that we do, does it not seem presumptuous to attempt to limit the power of the Almighty?

Can one decide without possibility of a mistake what God would desire to do? If God can perform a miracle and might desire to do so, it becomes merely a matter of evidence, and the Bible evidence is sufficient for those who accept the Bible as the word of God. Our difficulty is chiefly with those who declare that God cannot, or will not, perform a miracle.

The Boast of Materialism.

Materialism is the source of most of the doubt entertained by this generation on the subject of miracles. Its attractiveness lies largely in the boast that it brings nature within the limits of human reason by eliminating all that is mysterious. It is built upon the idea of unity, an unbroken chain of cause and effect. It flatters the mind to be told that there is nothing that it cannot understand.

Materialism cannot explain why a raven would carry food to a man; therefore, the materialist denies that it did. Neither can materialism explain why a man would travel a long way to a brook and expect ravens to feed him; therefore, the materialist denies that he did. And, going back another step, materialism cannot explain why God would tell Elijah to go to the brook and then send the ravens to feed him; therefore the materialist denies that He did.

By the same process of reasoning, materialism is unable to explain why Elijah appeared at this particular time and why he expressed himself so specifically on the weather; therefore, the materialist denies that he did.

Elijah's knowledge of the weather is one of the most difficult subjects that the materialist has to deal with, for man has not evolved much knowledge in regard to the weather.

Man Cannot Control the Weather.

We have weather stations scattered over the world, connected by wire and wireless, so that notice can be given of the coming of a storm, but the notice is not absolutely reliable. It simply means that a storm is now traveling over a certain area in a certain direction at a certain velocity and that if it keeps on in the same direction at the same speed and does not go up or around or stop, it will reach a certain point at a certain time.

The head of the weather bureau, so the story goes, called up President-elect Taft the night before his inauguration in 1909 and predicted nice weather for March 4. A little later a storm stole in from the east, and Inauguration Day was the worst in years.

If the Bible is to be believed, Elijah forecasted the

weather.   He predicted a drought and it came; he was told where to go, and he went.

When the brook dried up he was instructed to go to a widow's house and find food.   He obeyed, and he found the widow to whose home he had been sent, but the poor woman was in no position to feed a stranger. When he asked her for food she explained to him very frankly that she had but a little meal in a jar and but a little oil in a cruse; she was gathering fuel that she might cook the remnant of oil and meal and eat it with her son and then die.

Elijah asked her to prepare his food first and assured her that the meal and oil would not give out until succor came.   Worshipper of Baal though she was, she obeyed the command of God's prophet and it was even as he had said.

Here we have another miracle.   Materialism cannot explain how Elijah could know that the meal and the oil could continue to feed three people without being exhausted, any more than it can explain how a bush could be burning without being consumed, or how a voice could come out of the bush and summon Moses to one of the greatest tasks in history.

While the drought was yet over the land, the widow's son was stricken with death.   In her anguish she was ready to attribute his death to the presence of Elijah, but when the prophet called back the vital spark and restored the son to the mother she recognised in him a man of God.

Human Beings as God's Messengers.

We might see in the service rendered by Elijah an illustration of " bread cast upon the waters," or of the " entertaining of angels unawares."   But this unexpected return for kindness done is so frequent that it does not need the experience of Elijah to impress it. No one who has reached mature years is without corroborative experience.

That is one of the practical things about the Christian spirit. It is not calculating, and yet its arithmetic is more accurate than the calculation of the selfish. Those who never do any good until they stop to calculate whether it will return to them, spend time figuring that they ought to spend acting. Those who do good as opportunity offers are sowing seed all the time and they need not doubt the harvest.

But the great lesson that we are to draw from these incidents in the life of Elijah is that God uses human beings as His messengers. He selects them, qualifies them for the work and sends them forth to proclaim His truth. He supplies His agents with power from the Almighty's exhaustless storehouse, and establishes their authority by such proofs as He deems proper. This He has done throughout the ages. He gives strength for the tasks that are delegated to them and guards them from dangers until their work is done.

" Here Am I; Send Me."

This is the Bible story as embodied in this lesson on Elijah. Is it true or false? Those who believe it is true find it is easy to understand the Bible, and its lessons will be sufficient for them in every time of need and under all circumstances. Those who believe the story is false will read the Bible in vain; its precepts will have no binding force with them.

Believing the Bible account to be true, I present it as it is written. It makes a personal appeal to each of us; we do not know in advance to what work God may call us, but every day, everywhere, there is work to be done. The Heavenly Father has business for us all, labour suited to our strength and faith. From among those whose hearts are wholly His and who sincerely say, as Elijah could say, " Here am I, send me," He will select those best fitted to carry out His will.

XIV

ELIJAH: THE PROPHET OF FIRE

I KINGS 18: 20-24, 30, 36-39

THE things it tells of happened twenty-eight hundred years ago, yet how crammed with lessons for us of today is the eighteenth chapter of the first book of Kings!

It continues the fascinating story of Elijah, begun with such startling suddenness in the previous short chapter. He had appeared before Ahab, wickedest of the kings of the ten tribes of Israel, and foretold a drought as punishment for the nation's sin of idolatry, introduced by Jezebel, the king's strong-minded consort. Then, as mysteriously as he had come, he had vanished and been fed by ravens, in the morning and in the evening, and from the widow's barrel of meal that wasted not and the cruse of oil that did not fail. And all the time there was sore famine throughout Samaria.

"And it came to pass after many days, that the word of the Lord came to Elijah in the third year, saying, Go, shew thyself unto Ahab; and I will send rain upon the earth."

The Lesson of Obadiah.

As Elijah journeyed towards Ahab's capital he met Obadiah, the governor of the king's house, who not only feared the Lord greatly, but also feared Ahab. When Jezebel, worshipper of Baal, was slaying the prophets of Israel, he had been loyal enough to the Almighty God to save one hundred of them and hide them in caves and feed them; but when Elijah told him to go and announce to Ahab his coming, Obadiah trembled and explained to the prophet that he was afraid to do so lest Elijah might vanish again, and then his life would pay the penalty for a seemingly false report to the king.

There is so much meat in our chapter that we cannot devote much time to Obadiah or to the hundred prophets who hid in caves, although this part of it has been used as a basis for comment on the lack of courage sometimes displayed by ministers who hide from the wrath of the unrighteous instead of upbraiding them.

But allowance must be made for the difference in the intensity of convictions. Some have conviction enough for ordinary times; others have convictions enough for every emergency. Such characters as Elijah are valuable, therefore, as a reproof to those who are weak in the faith and as a stimulus to those who have to meet great trials. The progress of Christianity is slow because the spirit of the martyrs is not to be found in all who profess faith in God—not even in all who openly take upon themselves the Name of His Son.

An Example of Supreme Courage.

When Elijah met Ahab, the latter, who had searched everywhere for the prophet and had even demanded an oath of the kingdoms where he failed to find him, gave expression to his anger in words that have become historic: " Art thou he that troubleth Israel? "—an accusation and a compliment. Why had he hunted far and wide for Elijah? Because he believed that Elijah was the spokesman of the Almighty and that the drought which lay over his kingdom could not be broken until word came from Elijah. He charged Elijah with troubling Israel and yet he knew that Elijah was the only one through whom relief could be brought.

Elijah's answer was in keeping with the character of that great man of God. "I have not troubled Israel; but thou, and thy father's house, in that ye have forsaken the commandments of the Lord, and thou hast followed Baalim."

"Thou art the man!" There is courage! An unarmed prophet of Jehovah—all the rest of them had been destroyed or driven into hiding, but here is one whom neither the frown of the king nor the king's armies could terrify. He had not waited until Ahab found him, but went himself to the king and, hurling back Ahab's reproach, uttered before Ahab God's indictment of his idolatry.

The Choice That All Must Make.

Then follows the greatest prayer test recorded in history—one of the most sublime acts of faith ever displayed by man.

Taking command of the situation, Elijah ordered Ahab to assemble the prophets of Baal, four hundred and fifty in number, unto Mount Carmel, and when these leaders of the idolaters assembled Elijah spoke unto the people, who had gathered to witness the scene. "How long halt ye between two opinions!" he exclaimed. "If the Lord be God, follow him; but if Baal, then follow him."

This is a practical lesson because it touches every

human life. This is the choice that all are called upon to make. From the time we reach years of account-ability until we die, this is the choice that we are continually making—choice between God and Baal, between the Heavenly Father and the false gods that invite worship—and success or failure follows accord-ing to the decision.

Elijah did not allow much time for them to make up their minds, and but little time is required for this choice. The decisions upon which our lives turn are made in a moment; whether we turn to the right or to the left, we act instantly.

We may spend time in considering the matter, in pondering over it, but only a moment is required for the decision, whether it is to become a murderer, a thief, or a criminal of any other kind. And it requires no longer to decide, as did the Prodigal Son, " I will arise and go to my father."

Elijah's Sublime Trust in God.

The people stood mute before Elijah; "answered him not a word." Then the prophet proposed the test.

" I, even I only, remain a prophet of the Lord; but Baal's prophets are four hundred and fifty men." He challenged them to bring two bullocks, they to choose one and put it on an altar with no fire under it; he would take the other bullock and do likewise. Then the prophets of Baal were to call upon their gods to send down fire from heaven to consume the sacrifice, and he would call upon Jehovah; "and the God that answereth by fire, let him be God."

Imagine, if you can, a more sublime picture of trust in God! Not only was Elijah's own life staked upon the result, but the faith of the children of Israel also.

He let the prophets of Baal make their appeal first—another evidence of faith. If they had succeeded, he would not have been given a chance to call down fire upon the offering he had prepared. And the prophets of Baal tried; they had but little choice, of course, and could not well refuse. They were brought together by the command of Ahab, who summoned them in obedience to the demand of Elijah. Standing in the presence of the people, they had to take the chance or confess the impotence of their god.

Atheists and Higher Critics.

But they must be given credit for a larger faith than those have who today call the Bible a man-made book. If uninspired men made the Old and New Testaments, why do not uninspired men prepare another Bible? If the Bible is a man-made book, surely men ought to be able to make a better book today than our Bible. But the atheist has not as much faith in his doctrines as the prophets of Baal twenty-eight hundred years ago had in their god, for the atheist will not attempt the making of a substitute for the Bible.

Baal did not answer and then Elijah gave additional proof of the completeness of his trust. He ridiculed the prophets of Baal, mocked them before he himself had appealed to his God. No man with the slightest doubt would have taken the risk of laughing at his rivals before the contest was over, but Elijah had unquestioning faith and he dared to ridicule the efforts of the worshippers of a false god, just as today the believers in a personal God, in an inspired Book and in a deified Christ mock those who would make the Creator impersonal, the Bible a story-book and Christ a mere man.

THE PROPHET OF FIRE   111

Then came Elijah's opportunity, and here again his faith shines forth. He was not content to call down fire upon dry wood as the prophets of Baal tried to do. He had the wood saturated three times with barrels of water—possibly the materialists think it was oil in disguise, but the spectators did not. Elijah prayed, and what a modest prayer it was: " Let it be known this day that thou art God in Israel, and that I am thy servant, and that I have done all these things at thy word."

The Power of Prayer With Faith.

Elijah was the conduit through which the power of God flowed; he was the instrument in Jehovah's hand. Could humility be better expressed?

He was not thinking of himself, but of the children of Israel: " Hear me, O Lord, hear me, that this people may know that thou art the Lord God, and that thou hast turned their heart back again."

A recent writer, a professing Christian, assumed to divide the miracles into two groups, the individual to make the classification for himself. In one group would be the recorded miracles for which there seemed (to the individual) to be no sufficient reason; in the other group would be the miracles that might be justified (according to the judgment of the individual) as necessary to produce an effect worth producing. Even according to this ridiculous classification, Elijah's prayer test would seem worth while. It was intended to destroy faith in idol worship which Jezebel was introducing and to take the heart of the children of Israel back to the God of Abraham, Isaac, and of Israel.

" Then the fire of the Lord fell, and consumed the burnt sacrifice, and the wood, and the stones, and the dust, and licked up the water that was in the trench.

And when all the people saw it, they fell on their faces; and they said, The Lord, he is the God; the Lord, he is the God."

We are surprised at the short-lived faith of a chosen people; amazed that it was so often necessary to coerce them into reverence and obedience by visible acts of power and authority, but why should we wonder? Even today there are people—so-called learned people even—who do not believe. They not only laugh at what they call " the fables of the Bible," but they reject evidence far more conclusive than that which existed in the days of Elijah.

We know of the vastness of the universe and of the myriad forms of life, each perfect in its mechanism and unquestioning in its obedience to the law woven into its very being. We see the wonder-working of a Power that is measureless, designs that could only come from an Infinite Intelligence, and a bounty that bespeaks the fathomless love of a Heavenly Father. We have the experience of the ages and proof of Christ's power to regenerate a world; and yet even now it sometimes requires a catastrophe to turn the wandering heart back to Jehovah. The great lesson of this study teaches the need of an unwavering faith in an unchanging God.

XV

AHAB: THE COVETOUS KING

I KINGS 21 : 7-10, 16-20

HOW human are the Bible's greatest characters!
Here is Elijah. With incomparable courage, he had dared upbraid Israel's king for his
idolatry. Facing alone the four hundred and fifty
prophets of Baal, he had proven their god false in the
greatest prayer test recorded in history. As punishment for leading the ten tribes of Israel from the worship of the Almighty God, he had put those priests of
Baal to the sword.

But when word came to him from Ahab's idolatrous
queen Jezebel that she would have his life on the mor-
row, he forgot his faith in the Almighty and fled in
dismay—ran into the wilderness and, in despair, sat
down to rest under a juniper tree. There he came to
himself long enough to feel the sting of remorse. He
was ashamed of his cowardice and, recognising his
weakness, wanted to die.

God Does Not Desert Us.

It was an act dramatically inconsistent with the rest
of Elijah's life—yet how human! In considering it, it
must be remembered that he was not only frightened
but weary. He had undergone a severe trial. His contest of faith with the followers of Baal had been long
drawn out, and then he had run before Ahab for
eighteen miles to the gates of Jezreel. The flesh is

sometimes weak when the heart is willing. And he was temporarily without anything to do.

But God did not desert Elijah, just as He does not desert us when we flee to the wilderness in our weak moments; He had other tasks not yet disclosed.

An angel awakened the prophet and put food before him. After he was refreshed he slept again, and again food was provided for him. In his restored strength he traveled forty days and forty nights unto Horeb, the mount of God. There he lodged in a cave, still fearful of the wrath of Jezebel. And there the word of the Lord came unto him in the inquiry, " What doest thou here, Elijah? "

Poor Elijah! How natural was his reply. He made the best excuse he could, and to the average man it seems a reasonable one.

He explained that he had been jealous for the Lord God of Hosts and for the Children of Israel, and this was not more than the truth. He felt that he was alone and that his life was in danger. He had suddenly plunged from exaltation to despair. No wonder he forgot to take a census of the faithful. There were seven thousand who had not bowed the knee to Baal, plain people who had not been so ecstatic in victory or so cast down in defeat. They are the ones who steady the boat in the storm.

The Still, Small Voice.

The Lord summoned Elijah again, sent him upon the mount and taught him a great lesson that has been of unspeakable value to all the generations since that day.

Elijah represented rugged strength; the strong arm of the Lord was made manifest through him. But now he was taught that God was not always in the wind, nor in the earthquake, nor in the fire, but that He was also in the still, small voice. Then the Lord gave Elijah other work to do, and with new tasks his strength returned.

I am not sure that we will find many lessons of more practical importance than this: Keep busy. As " Satan finds some mischief, still, for idle hands to do," so human weakness besets us most between our tasks. As sins abound in the nights that separate the days of toil, so our periods of discouragement and doubt lurk in the dark intervals between our seasons of activity.

When Elijah fled from the presence of Ahab's queen he had finished the work that God had put upon him, and no call had come to new acts of consecration, but just as soon as he heard the familiar voice of the Heavenly Father sending him on a new mission he went boldly about the Father's business.

A Covetous King.

And so we come to another great Bible lesson—Naboth's vineyard. A wonderful picture! A covetous king and the man of God meet again—this time in a murdered man's vineyard.

Ahab coveted the vineyard of Naboth—not an unusual thing. Many a man has conceived the idea of rounding out his garden by the purchase of adjoining land. And Ahab proceeded in quite a natural and unobjectionable way.

He spoke to Naboth about it, explaining his reason for desiring it. It was suitable for a garden of herbs and near to the king's house. He offered in exchange a better vineyard or, if Naboth preferred, he would pay him the worth of it in money. So far, so good.

The king may not have thought of any objections that Naboth could have. He may have felt that he was doing all that could be expected, and even more, but to Naboth the place had a sentimental value. He prized it as an inheritance from his fathers. The courtiers of the king could hardly understand how any one could refuse so fair a request as that made by Ahab. But the land belonged to Naboth, and he was entirely within his rights when he preferred to keep it rather than to sell it or take another place in exchange.

Thus far the story is not unlike many that have been written or might be written.

Jezebel's Conspiracy.

But Ahab was provoked and, like a spoiled child, threw himself down upon his bed and sulked, refusing to eat.

It was not long before his conduct was reported to Jezebel and she hastened to inquire why he was sad. He frankly explained to her the grievous disappointment that he had suffered and then his wicked wife gave him a lesson in the exercise of authority. She bade him eat and be merry, assuring him that she would give him Naboth's vineyard. Then she proceeded to frame a conspiracy against Naboth.

Addressing the elders and nobles who lived in his city, she ordered them to proclaim a feast and set Naboth in the chief place. Then, by her direction, two base men, sons of Belial, were to be seated before Naboth with instructions to bring false witness against him.

The conspiracy was carried out to the letter. The fast was arranged, Naboth was put in the place of honour, the false witnesses appeared, made their lying accusations, and Naboth was carried out of the city and stoned to death.

"Hast Thou Found Me, O Mine Enemy?"

Then these willing accomplices in the murder of Naboth reported their success to Jezebel and she immediately conveyed the glad news to the king. He rose up and hurried down to the vineyard to take possession of it. When he arrived he met Elijah for the third time, the same Tishbite who warned him of the coming drought and then commanded him to summon the prophets of Baal to Mount Carmel for the prayer test. The prophet appeared before him at the command of the Almighty. Elijah was himself again—he was God's spokesman.

The scene lends itself to the artist, and it is not strange that it has been put upon the canvas. The staging is perfect.

There is the coveted garden; the former owner being dead, it became the property of the king according to a law, that Jezebel doubtless understood, giving the land to the king when the owner was put to death for blasphemy. In the midst of the garden stands the king, wicked enough to enjoy the fruits of a victory bought by a murder that he was too cowardly to commit. Before him stands Elijah, stern voice of an offended God.

Ahab does not wait for Elijah to speak: his conscience accuses him before the prophet has time to hurl Jehovah's judgment at him. "Hast thou found me, O mine enemy?" exclaims the king! It is not necessary that one should be a king in order to stand, conscience-stricken, before the evidence of his guilt. It is conscience that, as Shakespeare says, "makes cowards of us all."

The outstanding lesson of this incident is the sin of covetousness. Possibly nowhere else is the importance of the Tenth Commandment so emphasised. It comes last, but it is by no means least in importance. It is so intimately connected with all the others relating to man's dealing with his fellow man that its observance is of the very first importance.

The Beginning of Evil.

In this case, covetousness led to false witness, to murder, and to theft. Covetousness would be better understood if the visible masks under which it operates did not divert attention from it. When one steals, attention is centered upon the act, although covetousness is concealed behind it. When one commits murder it is often due to covetousness, although the covetousness is hidden. False witness, too, is often but the outward manifestation of an inward covetousness.

It is the beginning of evil, and the beginning is the thing that needs most to be watched. Sin is not difficult to deal with if taken at its inception; it becomes a serious problem when it ripens into action.

Christ gave the only sure cure. He taught that the heart should be full of love to God—" Thou shalt love the Lord thy God with all thy heart, and with all thy soul, and with all thy mind, and with all thy strength." No vacuum must be left in the heart for evil thoughts to fill. When the heart is full it overflows, and the overflowing heart is the symbol of a Christian life.

The Real Cure for Covetousness.

But there is a second commandment that follows naturally after that which Christ declared to be the first and great commandment, namely, " Thou shalt love thy neighbour as thyself." That is the real cure for covetousness; or, rather, it prevents the birth of covetousness.

All kinds of wrongdoing follow in the wake of covetousness. When one starts out to do evil he never knows what crime he must commit to carry out his purpose: one evil step leads to another until he finds that "the wages of sin is death." On the other hand, no one knows what unexpected pleasures he may invite when he travels the path of righteousness.

Obedience to the First Commandment, "Thou shalt have no other gods before me," would have saved Ahab the experiences that he had at Mount Carmel. Obedience to the last would have saved him from the humiliation visited upon him in the vineyard.

"Keep thy heart with all diligence; for out of it are the issues of life."

XVI

NAAMAN: THE LEPER

II KINGS 5: 1-4, 9-14

OUR cast of characters, if we may so speak, include Elisha, the prophet; Naaman, the captain of the hosts of the king of Syria; a little Israelitish maiden, brought captive from Samaria, and a group described as Naaman's servants. All play important parts in the narrative.

Elisha needs no special description here. Naaman does. We are told that he was a great man with his master, that he was honourable because, by him, Jehovah had given victory unto Syria, and that he was a mighty man of valour—quite a string of titles, each one indicating distinction and, taken together, very impressive.

At the conclusion of the description of Naaman we find four words connected with his titles by the word "but"—"but he was a leper." These words cast a shadow over his life. No matter how high he stood in military affairs, no matter how close he was to the king, no matter what honours he had won, no matter how great his valour, his disease outweighed them all because it was incurable.

A Little Captive Maiden.

Enters now the little maiden; she waited on Naaman's wife. The Syrians had gone out in bands, as was customary in that day, and had carried her off captive. She was a servant in the house, and her master's affliction touched her heart. One day she ventured to tell her mistress that there was a prophet in Samaria who could heal the leprosy of Naaman.

If the suggestion had been made about other matters it might have received little attention, but any remedy is worth trying when all else has failed, so the word was immediately taken to the captain of the king's host, and Naaman seems to have acted at once. He called for his horses and his chariots and hurried to the house of Elisha.

The little girl, having played her part, disappears from the story. Naaman offers himself to Elisha as a patient, and, behold, the prophet, instead of hurrying out and showing courtesy to a high official coming in state, sends a message to him, saying: " Go and wash in the Jordan seven times, and thy flesh shall come again to thee, and thou shalt be clean."

Naaman was wroth. He turned away in indignation and complained of the manner in which he had been treated.

He had pictured to himself the prophet coming out to meet him—possibly wearing the mantle he had received from Elijah. He expected Elisha to call on Jehovah and wave his hand over the leprosy. But Naaman did not even get sight of the prophet.

To add insult to injury, he was sent to a river which, to Naaman, seemed far inferior to the rivers of Damascus. And, judging by appearance, Naaman was right.

Abana and Pharpar are beautiful streams; they burst out in springs from the base of the Lebanons and, flowing for a few miles, sink into the sands of the desert beyond Damascus. The Jordan is not nearly so inviting a stream, especially when it is high. When I visited Damascus and the Holy Land I recalled the words of Naaman and was not surprised at the comparison which he made. " So he [Naaman] turned and went away in a rage."

And now the servants come upon the stage. " His servants came near, and spake unto him, and said, ' My father, if the prophet had bid thee do some great thing, wouldest not thou have done it? How much rather, then, when he saith to thee, Wash and be clean ' ?"

The text does not tell us whether Naaman thanked the servants for thinking of such a sensible course when he had overlooked it. But, as in the case of the suggestion of the first servant, the little captive maiden, he followed the advice, went down and " dipped himself seven times in the Jordan; and his flesh came again like unto the flesh of a little child, and he was clean."

These are the facts of this beautiful story which has carried its many lessons to millions of lives.

God's Mysterious Ways.

First: " God moves in a mysterious way, His wonders to perform."

A little girl, carried against her will into the land of the enemy, becomes the messenger of God to spread a knowledge of His power among those who knew Him not. Christianity was scattered over wide areas by the violence of hostile governments, but wherever it went it made its impression. Daniel went as a captive to Babylon and became the adviser to the king. Joseph was sold in Egypt and won his way from a dungeon to a place by the side of Pharaoh. From prison cells God's truth has been proclaimed from the days of Paul to Bunyan's time.

And so a little girl, serving the mistress of a mighty man of valour, captain of the king's host, was the evangelist who carried into the household, and through it to the king's palace, and afterwards to the whole world, knowledge of the fact that there is a God and that He speaks to man through His prophets.

Note how little circumstances form links in the chain of events.

The invasion of Samaria may have been the whim of some military chieftain; this little girl was only one of many from whom captives might have been selected, and Naaman's house was doubtless but one of the many supplied with captured servants. If any one of many circumstances had been wanting, the story would have been different, but they combined to bring a noted patient to the house of a Man of God.

Naaman's Lesson in Humility.

We never know which one of the multitude of little acts that fill up our days will prove a turning point in our lives or the lives of others. We do not see life in its entirety and, therefore, cannot know which act will bring the largest fruitage.

But this we know: If a noble purpose runs through all that we do; if all the duties of each day are done in the right spirit, ours will be an honourable part wherever our lives touch the lives of others. Because we do not know when our light will be a guide to some one in need, our lamps must always be trimmed and burning.

Second: Naaman expected too much—it was natural that he should. He was a big man in the government and respect was shown him by all below his rank. It never occurred to him that a private citizen of another land would so far ignore his station as to send an answer by a servant.

Elisha taught him a lesson in humility. Naaman learned that the spokesman of the Almighty is above all earthly potentates. It was a hard lesson to learn, but he learned it. The materialists among our scientists might take this lesson to heart. They should not look down upon those who deal with spiritual things.

Third: Naaman also learned not to judge by appearances.

The washing that he needed was not the kind for which ordinary water was sufficient. The waters of Abana and Pharpar were sparkling and inviting to the eye, but they did not have the healing power of the waters of Jordan, and Jordan's waters would have brought no relief but for the fact that God had given to them a healing power for this occasion. Naaman found that God, who made all things, could use anything that He had made—use as He wanted to use it and make it fulfill His purpose.

Fourth: Naaman learned another important lesson, probably the most important that *we* shall gather from these verses, namely, not to rely too much on the things that are spectacular and impressive. If he had been told to do some great thing it would have seemed in keeping with his own greatness, but to do a little thing —seemingly trivial—was beneath him.

And may we not be in danger of making the same mistake? Lives are often wasted in waiting for big opportunities. "Despise not the day of small things," is a wise admonition. The simple things of life are the foundation upon which great achievements are built. Little things grow into big things, just as vegetables develop from tiny seeds and mighty oaks from little acorns. We use the small tasks as stepping stones to the large accomplishments of life.

Fifth: Naaman learned, too, that people cannot think straight when they are angry. He felt offended and then acted while his blood was hot. " He was wroth " and " in a rage."

It was fortunate that he did not do worse than he did. A mighty man of valour is sometimes dangerous when he is mad. Nations have been plunged into war by rulers when they were angry. Millions of lives have been sacrificed because of actions inspired by men who were in a rage. When a man is angry he swaggers about and talks about what he can do; when he is calm he considers what he ought to do. It is well to postpone action until reason resumes its sway. Our nation has negotiated thirty treaties, the chief merit of which is the cooling-off time given for deliberation before action.

Sixth: Naaman was taught still another lesson—that he could learn from those whom he regarded as his inferiors. He would have gone away unhealed had not his servants advised him against rashness. They gave him a little, every-day common sense and Naaman was wise enough to accept it and act upon it.

We get a great deal from others; in fact, nearly all we know. No one has a monopoly of wisdom—no person and no age. Wisdom passed from generation to generation, even before the printed page brought it within the reach of all.

We never know when we are going to get an idea, or where we are going to get it, or what we are going to do with it, or what it is going to do with us. Naaman's servants gave him some homely advice; he followed it, and now it belongs to the world. Indignant as he was, he saw, on reflection, that the sensible thing was to do what he was told to do.

Finally: Naaman learned the great lesson of obedience. It was ʰildish of him to question " Why? " " Are not the rivers of Damascus better than all the waters of Israel? " He had traveled all the way from home to the house of Elisha; he had gone to the only one of whom he knew who could heal him. Why should he refuse to follow the simple instructions to which the Man of God attached the promise of relief?

Mystery That Is Immaterial.

And why should we disobey? The world is full of mystery, but about things that are immaterial. The necessary things are easy to understand.

The very life that we live is mysterious; we cannot understand it, but we can live. The food that we eat is mysterious; we cannot understand how it grows, but we can eat it, and it sustains life.

So God is a mystery: our finite minds cannot comprehend Him, but we can believe in Him because we see on every hand evidences of His power and His love.

The Bible may contain passages which are not clear to us, but that which all can understand, even the most ignorant, is sufficient to furnish us an infallible guide through life.

And so with Christ. We are so imperfect that we may find it hard to comprehend His perfection; our powers are so limited that we may not be able to understand His plenitude of power; but we can understand all that is necessary to our salvation. We can wash in His blood and be clean. We can accept Him, follow Him and enjoy the abundant life which He reveals.

XVII

ELISHA: "THE MAN OF GOD"

II Kings 6:8-17

IN this chapter we are to deal with a noted incident in the life of the prophet Elisha, again and again described in the Bible as "the man of God." But first a few words about the fate of a faithless servant.

Naaman, captain of the king's host, and a great man in Syria, had been healed of leprosy by Elisha. He had importuned his benefactor to accept the rich gifts which he had brought with him out of Syria, and Elisha had steadfastly refused.

But when Naaman and his retinue had departed a little way, the plan came to Gehazi, Elisha's servant, to turn to his own advantage the gratitude that the Syrian captain felt toward his master. He ran after Naaman and, making up a lie, represented the prophet as having reconsidered his refusal to the extent of accepting a talent of silver and two changes of raiment for two sons of the prophets who had arrived unexpectedly.

Of course, Naaman was only too glad to comply with the request, supposedly from Elisha. He gave Gehazi the two changes of raiment, and he urged upon him two talents of silver instead of one.

When Gehazi returned, Elisha greeted him with a question that showed he knew what had been done, and then he called down upon Gehazi and his posterity the leprosy of which Naaman had been healed. "And he went out from his presence a leper as white as snow."

The lesson of Gehazi is obvious. He who betrays a trust brings harm not only to himself but to the innocent as well. As no man can live unto himself, so none can sin unto himself.

Lepers of Modern Life.

The business man who lies to gain an advantage over a competitor; the banker who misappropriates funds entrusted to his keeping; the public servant who uses the people's confidence in him to line his pockets with graft—all are Gehazis of modern life. And the terrible punishment that is theirs when, their sins at last found out, they stand in the presence of those they betrayed as lepers white as snow!

Now it came to pass that the king of Syria, warring against Israel, discovered that all of his plans became known to the king of Israel. Whenever Benhadad called his captains together and planned the campaign for the next day, Elisha would communicate the plans of the enemy to the Israelitish king, and with this knowledge he was able to escape from the traps set for him.

Benhadad naturally concluded that there was a traitor in his camp and called his servants together that he might find out the guilty party. One of his servants explained that Elisha was able to tell the king of Israel even the words spoken in the bedchamber of the king of Syria.

A Memorable Answer.

Then Benhadad started out to capture the prophet. He sent horses and chariots and a great host; by night they encamped about the city in which Elisha dwelt.

In the morning Elisha's servant saw that the city was surrounded and went in alarm to his master with the question, "How shall we do?"

Elisha answered with these memorable words, "Fear not, for they that be with us are more than they that be with them."

This is the faith that saves from fear. It is the perfect trust that casteth out fear; it is the secret of that courage which nothing can shake.

Elisha prayed that the eyes of his servant might be opened. "And the Lord opened the eyes of the young man; and he saw; and, behold, the mountain was full of horses and chariots of fire round about Elisha."

This is just such a defense as David speaks of in the thirty-fourth Psalm, "The angel of the Lord encampeth round about them that fear him, and delivereth them."

Elisha's servant had made his calculations on the basis of the things that were visible—his were the estimates that are common to those who lack faith in God's justice, in God's power, and in God's willingness to succor those who fight His battles.

Pharaoh was as blind as Elisha's servant; it never occurred to him that there was any way of escape for the children of Israel. The Red Sea was before them and the Egyptians were following with horses and chariots.

To every eye except the eye of faith the end seemed near for God's chosen people, but Pharaoh was ignorant of the plans of Jehovah—so ignorant that his soldiers followed the fleeing Israelites when the sea opened for their escape. Destiny was not disclosed until Moses and his followers had reached the farther shore and the waves closed over their pursuers.

Time and again that which seemed to be destiny has
been turned into disaster, and that which looked like
defeat has been converted into victory by some unexpected happening.   A storm scatters the Spanish
Armada and the history of Europe is changed for
centuries; a sunken road at Waterloo turns the tide of
battle and Napoleon goes to St. Helena instead of
becoming the military master of the world.

The Unseen Hosts of Right.

Here is an important lesson of our study—unseen
hosts fight on the side of righteousness; God's invisible
army waits in reserve to bring victory to His side.

Not in great crises in history only, but every day and
in every life, faith can, in man's extremity, summon
light and reinforcements from the Almighty's exhaustless storehouse.

" Faith in the wisdom of doing right " is a practical
virtue.   It is this faith that leads God's servants to
attempt the seemingly impossible; they rely upon infinite wisdom, love and power.   That is why one with
God shall chase a thousand and two put ten thousand
to flight.

We are traveling toward the dawn when we walk in
God's way.   He is our pillar of cloud by day and our
pillar of fire by night.   He gives us strength for every
hour of need.

" Thou Shalt Not Smite Them."

Elisha prayed that the Syrian army, sent to take him
for betraying Benhadad's movements to the king of
Israel, might be smitten with blindness and, his prayer
being answered, he went among the troops and offered
to lead them to the man whom they were seeking.

They followed him until they were in Samaria, the capital of Israel. Then their eyes were opened and they found that they were surrounded by the enemy's army.

Israel's king, elated at the success of Elisha's ruse, wanted to kill the Syrians. "My father, shall I smite them? Shall I smite them?" he eagerly asked. Note the answer of the prophet: "Thou shalt not smite them. Wouldest thou smite those whom thou hast taken with thy sword and with thy bow? Set bread and water before them, that they may eat and drink, and go to their master."

He made "great provision" for them and sent them away indebted to him for their lives as well as for food and drink.

Then follows a sentence that might well serve as a text, today, in every pulpit in Christendom: "So the bands of Syria came no more into the land of Israel."

Solomon put self-restraint above military achievements—"He that is slow to anger is better than the mighty; and he that ruleth his spirit than he that taketh a city." The world never needed more than it does today the spirit with which Elisha conquered the enemies of Israel.

The Only Foundation for Peace.

If the king of Israel had been permitted to carry out his plans of slaughter, there would have been retaliation and retaliation in return, and so on, generation after generation. The only way to put an end to war is to invoke the spirit that Elisha manifested, the spirit that Christ exemplified—the only spirit that can insure peace.

It is not a question of punishing the sins of the past;

there has been sin enough to justify any amount of punishment. But this story shows that the security of the future depends upon a change in the spirit of the world, and that change must begin with the substitution of love for hatred.

Friendship and co-operation are the only foundations upon which universal and perpetual peace can rest.

The old method—an eye for an eye—has been tried and found wanting.

The method that the prophet of God employed nearly three thousand years ago—the method that Christ taught in His life—is the only one for today. He proclaimed it from the Cross when He prayed, "Father, forgive them; for they know not what they do."

XVIII

JONAH: THE FIRST FOREIGN MISSIONARY

JONAH 3: 1-10

WHO is the first missionary of whom the Bible gives us an account?

Jonah; and, like all Bible biographies, his sets forth both his virtues and his faults.

The story, contained in the four short chapters of the Book of Jonah, begins with, " Now the word of the Lord came unto Jonah, the son of Amittai, saying, ' Arise, go to Nineveh, that great city, and cry against it; for their wickedness is come up before me.' "

But Jonah, instead of obeying the call, fled from the presence of the Lord, and at Joppa took ship for Tarshish. There follows the account of the storm sent by the Lord, " so that the ship was like to be broken "; the fear that came upon the sailors; the casting of lots, and the selection of Jonah as the one to blame for the tempest.

It must be said to Jonah's credit that in the hour of trial his conscience resumed command. He admitted his sin and was willing to be cast into the sea. The sailors hesitated, but finally choosing between the sacrifice of Jonah and their own safety, cast him overboard.

The Bible's Most Disputed Verse.

Then follows the one verse in all the Bible most frequently quoted by those who reject the miracles recorded in the Bible. If there is one miracle at which the skeptics scoff, it is the miracle that saved Jonah.

" Now the Lord had prepared a great fish to swallow up Jonah. And Jonah was in the belly of the fish three days and three nights."

Thus the first chapter of Jonah's biography ends.

" Then Jonah prayed unto the Lord his God out of the fish's belly." Thus the second chapter, which gives his prayer, begins; and it concludes with this verse:

" And the Lord spake unto the fish, and it vomited out Jonah upon the dry land."

The texts of our Talks so far this year have contained a record of numerous miracles, and the rejection of one is hardly possible except upon grounds that would lead to the rejection of all. Acceptance of some of these miracles requires a much stronger faith than is necessary for the acceptance of the miracle wrought for the rescue of Jonah.

Elijah's prayer test with the priests of Baal, for instance, and Elisha's raising from the dead of the son of the Shunammite woman—both of these are greater illustrations of the power of God manifested through His prophets. The sending of the ravens to feed Elijah and the healing of Naaman, captain of the hosts of Syria, of his leprosy were as clearly miraculous.

The Trouble With the Critics.

The trouble with those who reject the miracles is that they have adopted an hypothesis that precludes the miraculous. It is not, therefore, a question of proof with them, but what they regard as a matter of principle.

They profess to believe that miracles belittle the Almighty, and yet every one who has been born again knows of a miracle more mysterious than any recorded in Holy Writ. Some have characterised a miracle-working Jehovah as a " carpenter God," repairing the world from time to time by special acts of power. The theistic evolutionists picture God as having devised a plan by which the world unfolds according to a fixed law, each new development being the result of resident forces. But, however critics may differ in the treatment of other miracles, they unite in ridiculing the book of Jonah.

One of the most prominent of living higher critics has recently spoken lightly of the Bible account of the fish swallowing Jonah and then vomiting him up, and this, too, in spite of the fact that Christ uses the miracle of Jonah to illustrate His own burial of three days in the tomb. It requires some presumption on the part of a higher critic to set himself up as an authority on religion superior to the Saviour Himself, but some of them do not hesitate to do this.

Spiritual Dyspeptics.

The title " higher critic " is not a happy description of those to whom it is usually applied. In matters of religion they might better be called " dyspeptics." The Bible does not agree with them; they do not have the spiritual fluids in sufficient quantity to digest the miracle and the supernatural.

The higher critic above referred to who ridicules the account of Jonah, has no difficulty in endorsing the weird and fantastic explanations which spring from the imagination of Darwinists. In a recent book he says:

" Man has grown up in this universe gradually developing his powers and functions as responses to his environment. If he has eyes, so the biologists assure us, it is because light waves played upon the skin and eyes came out in answer; if he has ears, it is because the air waves were there first, and the ears came out to hear.

" Man never yet, according to the evolutionist, has developed any power save as a reality called it into being. There would be no fins if there were no water, no wings if there were no air, no legs if there were no land."

He can believe that the eye, the most wonderful of man's organs, could be brought into existence by light waves beating on the skin, and that the ear could be developed by sound waves (without deigning to explain why the light waves do not continue to bring out eyes and the sound waves to develop ears), but he cannot believe that the Creator of all things could send a particular fish to a particular place for a particular purpose. Darwinism seems to close the heart to spiritual truth and open the mind to the wildest guesses advanced in the name of science.

Prayer That Avails.

Those who reject the first and second chapters of Jonah will hardly be interested in the third with which the text for our Talk begins, but those who accept the Bible as true will see how a repentant man obeyed a second call and went to deliver God's message to Nineveh.

Nineveh was an exceeding great city and Jonah spoke with such earnestness that he converted the whole population. They proclaimed a fast and put on sackcloth from the greatest to the least.

Even the king hearkened to the message, laid aside

his royal robe, covered himself with sackcloth, (the coarse garment that indicated repentance), and sat in ashes. He issued a proclamation commanding that neither man nor beast should taste food or water.

It was a real revival, a sincere turning from sin and an appeal for mercy. They did not know whether God would repent and turn away from His fierce anger, but they felt that they must either touch the heart of the Almighty or perish.

This is the prayer that avails; it expresses faith in the power of God and faith in His loving kindness. It is the kind of repentance that makes it possible for God to blot out sin and remember it no more against the transgressor.

The Most Wicked Can Repent.

And the people prevailed with God. The Heavenly Father saw that they turned away from their evil way; " and God repented of the evil, that He had said He would do unto them; and He did it not."

The experience of Nineveh presents an impressive lesson. It was a wicked city and its wickedness threatened its destruction. But the most wicked can repent. They can turn from their sins and be forgiven. The wages of sin is death, but salvation is possible when the conditions are complied with.

God would not that any should perish and is quick to forgive. He is more willing to give good gifts unto His children even than earthly parents, and the greatest of all gifts is forgiveness.

The story of the Prodigal Son emphasises the continuing love of the Heavenly Father. It only waits an opportunity for expression, and repentance is the key that unlocks the reservoir of divine love. If a parent's heart can be touched by a child's repentance, why not the heart of the Heavenly Father?

We have in the story of Jonah three instances of repentance—the repentance of Jonah when he was punished for evading the call of the Lord; the repentance of a wicked city when it listened to the message of the prophet of Jehovah, and the repentance of God Himself when a city sincerely repents and the people turn from their wicked ways.

And the closing chapter of Jonah's biography tells how the prophet was provoked at the saving of Nineveh!

Having threatened the city with destruction, he sulks and complains when the Lord heard the prayer of the people and withheld the impending destruction.

God's Use of Our Weaknesses.

He was rebuked by a simple lesson, but we are not informed whether he was as open to suggestion as the people of Nineveh.

As he sat on the east side of the city, till he might see what would become of it, the Lord made a gourd to spring up quickly from the ground and cast its shadow over his head. And Jonah was glad for the gourd.

But the next day God smote the gourd, so that it withered. And Jonah was angry for the gourd.

" Then said the Lord, Thou hast had pity on the gourd, for which thou hast not laboured. . . . And should I not spare Nineveh, that great city, wherein are more than six score thousand persons that cannot discern between their right hand and their left hand? "

The narrative begins with Jonah's cowardice and ends with this account of his petulance, but between these two lamentable failures he manifests courage and spiritual power.   This combination of strength and weakness is not without its lesson to us.

God uses the material at hand; He does not call all in youth as He called Samuel, and all are not uniformly useful.   He can make use of all degrees of strength and can even use our weaknesses as a warning to others.

Jonah teaches us important lessons by the weaknesses that carry him down into the valley of despondency as well as by the virtues that shine forth when he was at his best.

XIX

AMOS: THE HERDSMAN-SEER

Amos 6: 1-8

YE, who pass your lives in ease, take heed, before it is too late, of the warning addressed to the children of Israel by the prophet Amos.

He was a herdsman of Tekoa, a village of Judæa, a few miles south of Bethlehem; like Elisha, he came from the common people. The former was at his plough when he was called to proclaim Jehovah's truth; the call came to Amos as he was tending his flocks.

Amos' message was not to a particular transgressor, like the message that Elijah carried to Ahab, the wicked king of Israel; nor did he, like Elisha, exercise miraculous power for the benefit of individuals. His was a proclamation to a people, an indictment against a nation —especially against those in a position of leadership.

He startled the worshippers of the god of ease—one of the earliest false gods. Altars were set up before this god in the very beginning of human history, and ever since multitudes have been his willing worshippers. If any one thinks that the first commandment was intended only for the children of Israel, he has read history in vain.

Love of Body vs. Love of God.

The gods of wood and stone were not the only menace to the morals of the children of Israel. To them, as to all others, came the temptations to give undue attention to the body, and from that day down to this millions have put love of the body above the love of God, and care for the body above care for the soul. A large part of our money, our time and our thought is expended on comforts for the body—often an extravagantly large part—and yet most of our temptations come through it and much of our sufferings. Christ warned against giving excessive attention to the body.

Where the means have been sufficient to permit idleness and mere physical enjoyment, lives have not only been made worthless, but they have been ruined by adoration of the god of ease. His worshippers eat, not because food is necessary to the body but because they enjoy eating; they sleep, not because the body needs sleep but because they like it.

They eat and eat and eat; they sleep and sleep and sleep; and then they rise up to eat and eat and eat again. They spend on food that which is needed for nobler purposes; they waste in idleness precious moments freighted with infinite possibilities of service. They know nothing higher than the flesh and its pleasures; they live as the brute lives and die without having obtained even a glimpse of the larger rewards.

A Common Source of Sin.

Amos bursts in upon a people given up to self-indulgence and, smiting with prophetic words, seeks to save them from the penalty that transgressions bring upon the guilty. It is a very complete indictment: "Woe to them that are at ease in Zion, and to them that are secure in the mountain of Samaria, the notable men of the chief of the nations."

Ease is sometimes the result of demoralisation—idleness following vices, but it is more often a cause. Carl Hilty, a Swiss writer, has declared that happiness is possible only when one is busy. He says the body must toil, the mind must be occupied, and the heart must be satisfied.

Virtue, too, is inconsistent with idleness. It is hardly possible for one to remain virtuous if he has nothing to do. The fact that he is willing to do nothing is proof of moral weakness, and where his idleness is not the fruit of a perverted heart it soon destroys the morals.

Amos singles out the notable men first—" chief of the nations." They have no more right to be at ease than the unidentified members of the mass, and their responsibility is even greater. As their example has influence, they not only harm society by withholding service, but they offend on a larger scale by leading others astray.

They also are the greatest losers. Many are so occupied with the necessities of life that they have little time for altruistic labours; they must feed and clothe themselves and take care of those immediately dependent upon them. If one by inheritance, by good fortune, or by his own ability has leisure time, he is able to devote that time to altruistic service and therefore taste the greater joys that flow from the satisfaction of spiritual impulses.

The Temptation to Live Luxuriously.

Amos brings a very specific indictment against the guilty—" that lie upon beds of ivory, and stretch themselves upon their couches." They yield to the temptation to live luxuriously. Money that might be spent for the hastening of God's kingdom and for the promotion of the general weal is lavished upon expensive beds. They are no more comfortable than other beds, but they please the eye and tickle the vanity. The money spent in high living often excites envy, creates discontent, and establishes barriers between those who should be friendly.

Continuing his indictment, Amos accuses the notables of eating "the lambs out of the flock, and the calves out of the midst of the stall." Not satisfied with "food sufficient for them," they must have the choicest lambs out of the flock and the fatted calves—their thoughts still on the body and their affections set on the things that please the palate. Few generations have been entirely without such, and in many generations these epicures have been numerous. It is well that we have an occasional reminder of the evils into which we are led when thought is centered upon the throat and attention absorbed in ministering to the taste.

Another count in Amos' indictment is that they "chant to the sound of the viol, and invent to themselves instruments of music"; and, indignant at such base imitation, he adds, "like David." I wonder if Amos would find any music today that would draw forth his invectives?

The Motto of the Sensualist.

Those of whom the prophet was speaking drank "wine in bowls," and anointed themselves with the "chief ointments." Not a symptom of degeneration was absent.

Their chief business was feeding themselves and filling themselves with wine. In the intervals between meals they anointed themselves with oil and stretched themselves upon their ivory beds. They were con-

cerned with their own pleasures, and they were not
" grieved for the affliction of Joseph." They were not
grieved for the affliction of anybody while they were
not afflicted themselves.

The body has no sentiment; it knows self and self
only. Just in proportion as the thought is centered on
the body, it is withdrawn not only from fellowship
with the world, but from fellowship with the soul, and
even with the mind. It is possible to become so devoted
to the body that intellectual pleasures have no attrac-
tion. " Eat, drink and be merry " is the motto of the
sensualist.

" Drinking wine in bowls " recalls the conditions that
existed in this country only a few years ago, and which
exist in some countries today. Less than a generation
ago wine was served in unlimited quantities at nearly
all public banquets of prominence. The charge was
five dollars, ten dollars, or even twenty-five dollars a
plate, the principal expense being for wine.

The banquet was divided into three parts. First,
eating and drinking—mostly drinking. Then followed
speaking—those speaking who were still able to speak.
Third, " the mopping up "—those who were sober took
the drunken ones from under the table, sorted them and
sent them home; and all said, " What a glorious night
we have had." Our public dinners are no longer riot-
ous affairs; after-dinner drunkenness has disappeared,
and banqueters find that genial companionship is possible without alcoholic stimulants.

God No Respecter of Persons.

Amos concludes his indictment of the ease worshippers of Israel with a prophecy: " Therefore, now shall
they go captive with the first that go captive, and the

revelry of them that stretched themselves shall pass away."

Here is a measure of justice which is not always administered in present day civilisation. The " notables " were to go captive with the first. Why not? Do not those sin most grievously who have the most light and who best understand the character of the crime? Should they not be punished first and most severely?

But it is not always so. Too often the social influence of the accused secures leniency, while the friendless prisoner receives the full penalty of the law. Amos spoke for the Almighty, and the Bible tells us that God is no respecter of persons. Prominence does not count in God's court. " Though hand join in hand, the wicked shall not be unpunished."

God, the prophet Amos proclaimed, abhorred the " excellency of Jacob," hated his palaces, and " would deliver up the city with all that is therein." In our next Talk we shall see that the prophecy was fulfilled. The moral of today's lesson is that the laws of God cannot be disobeyed with impunity.

Whether it be an individual who separates himself from the righteous and gives himself over to self-indulgence, or a nation that forgets God and descends to the brute level, punishment is inevitable. This is history so clearly written that no intelligent person can be excused for not knowing that the laws of God are sure.

Do We Deserve Amos' Rebuke?

It is our duty to examine ourselves and inquire whether we deserve the rebuke of Amos; whether our horizon extends beyond the fleshpots. If our hearts are set upon food and clothing and shelter, we may be sure that punishment will be our lot. And we are just as sure of punishment if for the body we substitute the mind, and do not rise above the level of intellectual joys.

There is a region still higher in which the soul holds sway. It is the only part of man that is fit to rule. It is the only sovereign under whose government men and nations are safe. When the soul is on the throne, the body is made an obedient subject, and in obedience finds life and health and happiness.

The mind likewise needs spiritual direction. Under the leadership of the soul it can roam at will throughout the universe and still be humble and reverent. Amos recorded in advance the punishment that would befall individuals and peoples which were led away from God.

JOASH: THE PROTECTED OF PROVIDENCE

II Kings 11 : 1-4, 11-17

THE story of the young prince Joash, as presented in our text, is a fascinating one. It recalls two other Bible stories, and it has innumerable illustrations in lives upon which the light of publicity has not been turned.

The narrative is a simple one.

Athaliah, the mother of Ahaziah, king of Judah, was the daughter of Ahab, king of Israel, and, probably, the daughter of Jezebel. If there is anything in blood, her life furnishes circumstantial evidence of kinship with one of the most wicked women known to history.

When her son Ahaziah, the king, was killed in the revolt of Jehu against Israel's king, Athaliah aspired to Judah's throne, and to make the way clear for the gratification of her ambition she set out to kill off all who were of the royal blood.

It so happened that Jehosheba, sister of the dead Ahaziah, heard of the plot and stole away the babe Joash from among the king's sons and hid him, with his nurse, in the bed-chamber—an empty room in the palace, where, according to custom, the mattresses and bed coverings were kept. In this way Joash escaped the death that came to the rest of the dead king's sons. Later, in some way not explained, the child was taken into the temple, and there, the account says, was hidden for six years "in the house of the Lord" while his wicked grandmother reigned over the land.

In the seventh year, Jehoiada, the high priest, who was an uncle of the young prince, called in the captains and the soldiers and, having placed guards in position to protect him, brought forth the king's son, put a crown upon his head, gave him the testimony and anointed him, while the people clapped their hands and shouted, "God save the king."

The End of the Usurper.

When the usurper Athaliah heard the noise her suspicions were aroused, and she hurried to the temple, "and, behold, the king stood by the pillar, as the manner was," with the princes and the trumpeters beside him. She heard the people rejoice and the trumpeters blow. Then, we are told, she rent her clothes and cried, "Treason! treason!"

But the high priest, Jehoiada, had the advantage over her. She was in the Lord's house, where he presided, and he had the army on his side. He did not allow her to be slain in the temple, but she was taken outside and put to death.

It is not necessary to dwell upon the wickedness of Athaliah. The history of monarchy is replete with such criminals; hers was the customary way of removing those who might be rivals to the throne. It is shocking today because we have passed beyond the time when such barbarity would be tolerated. There was a time when kings not only admitted such cruelties but boasted of them. On the walls of one of the temples in Egypt there is a carving which represents a king holding in one hand the plaited hair of a number of victims, while with the other hand, uplifted, he waves a lash as if to strike. Times have changed since those far-off days. A ruler who is wise and desires to keep his throne does not play the tyrant.

Providential Care.

The lesson that stands out from the narrative is that of providential care. An aunt risked her life to save the child Joash. Her blood would have paid the penalty had anyone betrayed to Athaliah the fact that Joash was in hiding, but Jehosheba was willing to die if necessary and so the child escaped.

One recalls the story of a dreamer whose brethren plotted to kill him and then were persuaded to substitute death by starvation in a lonely pit for outright murder. This was at the suggestion of Reuben, who hoped to rescue him later.

Here, again, chance played a vital part in the development of a great career. The Ishmaelitish merchants happened to come that way at an opportune time and the jealous brothers breathed a sigh of relief to find that they could rid themselves of their hated rival and yet not be guilty of taking his life. Circumstance followed circumstance until the chain of events dragged Joseph through a dungeon to the side of Pharaoh.

The mother of Moses is also recalled. Possibly because she previsioned the mission of her son, she hid the child in the bullrushes. Another woman, by accident or by divine suggestion, happened that way and was touched, not by the smile but the cries of the babe.

It is easy to explain the lingering of the sister near to watch the child, but not so easy to explain why the child's mother should have been accepted as a nurse. At any rate, Moses was raised in the court of Pharaoh and was prepared by the oppressor of his race for the task of securing their release. Those who believe in providential care find much encouragement in Joseph, Moses and Joash.

The Hour and the Man Meet.

Every great life that fits into and moulds a period is made up of a multitude of circumstances, the absence of any one of which would have changed the result. In many of these cases the individual is ignorant of the work for which his life is being shaped. His preparation has no seeming connection with a life plan or with the needs of some great emergency. But the hour and the man meet.

When some Goliath appears, David appears also, with just the skill that the occasion requires. When a new nation is to be launched in a new world, a Jefferson appears to write the Declaration of Independence and a Washington is at hand with the military skill necessary for a commander, with the executive ability necessary for a first President, and with the poise and discretion necessary to bring the antagonistic elements of his day into harmonious co-operation.

When the Union was threatened there was one man (he seemed to be the only one) whose life was a mixture of the North and the South, whose sympathies were broad enough to include the whole country, and whose calmness and serenity enabled him to look beyond the conflict to a nation preserved.

If we can see the hand of Providence shaping history through lives that are unconscious of the part for which they are being prepared, how much easier it is to understand the currents that are set in operation by prayer.

If every human being is a part of God's plan, as he

must be if there be a God, it is not unreasonable to believe that the Heavenly Father is willing to direct those who seek to know His will in order that they may obey.   It is impossible that a Heavenly Father such as the Bible describes should be deaf to the entreaties of His children.   And of all the gifts which we may assume Him willing to give, what would He give more gladly than guidance to those whose hearts are open to divine suggestion?

When Hearts Appeal to God.

If we cannot doubt God's willingness to answer prayer, we need only be sure that there are means of communication to be certain that the means will be employed.   Without attempting to enumerate these means or to show preference between possible means, attention can be called to one very obvious avenue for communication between the human and the divine.

Every human act is the result of a decision and this decision, though instantaneous, may exercise a vital influence upon one's life.   If, for instance, the temptation comes to steal, the decision determines whether one will remain honest or become a thief; and so with the temptation to kill or to commit any other sin.   The power that restrains one at this critical moment may be an emanation from God.   Is it unreasonable to believe that this power will respond to an appeal from the heart?   And so with the decision as to whether a good act shall be performed or aid extended.

There was a moment when Reuben decided to plead for the life of Joseph and a moment when the others yielded to the plea.   There was a moment when the Ishmaelitish merchants decided to come that way and a moment when the plans of Joseph's brothers were changed. There was a moment when Joseph decided to risk imprisonment rather than yield to sin, and there was a dream that flitted through the mind of the butler, the dream that brought Joseph to the attention of Pharaoh.

There was a moment when a suggestion came to the mother of Moses—a suggestion that did not seem to come to any other of the afflicted mothers of that day. And these suggestions continued to come at each turning point in the life of the great law-giver.

God Still Loves and Guides.

There was a moment in the life of Jehosheba when she decided to rescue the threatened child Joash. During the six years that followed there may have been moments when a similar decision was made in regard to him. It is not unreasonable to believe that the God who needed Joash could and did turn the purpose of the aunt in favour of the welfare of His ward.

Is it unreasonable to believe that God still lives, still loves and still guides? God needs servants to do His work, today, as in the days gone by, and servants need direction as much as they ever did in the past.

The child whom we can succor or save may be as important a part of God's plan as Joseph, or Moses, or Joash. As we ourselves have been the recipients of a care as affectionate and as tender as that which Jehosheba lavished upon her nephew, so our devoted interest may be as necessary to some of God's little ones as the care of others has been necessary to us.

We see but a small part of God's plan, but we have faith in the power and wisdom and love of the Heavenly Father who fits events together in the mosaic of our lives.

XXI

UZZIAH: THE VICTIM OF PRIDE

II Chronicles 26: 3-5, 15-21

UZZIAH is one of the most interesting of the many kings mentioned in the Old Testament. With one exception, he sat longer on the throne of David than any of Judah's rulers, and—a thing quite unusual—he was made king by decision of the people themselves.

"Sixteen years old was Uzziah when he began to reign, and he reigned fifty and two years in Jerusalem."

He was a man who seized upon, and used, new ideals. "And he made in Jerusalem engines, invented by cunning men, to be on the towers and upon the bulwarks, to shoot arrows and great stones withal." He became a great ruler. Under him the power of Judah was mightily increased. His name spread far abroad. And then, at the very apogee of his prosperity and fame, he gave to the world for all time a lesson in wilful conduct that none interested in Christian living can afford to ignore.

At first, the king, as our text tells us, "did that which was right in the sight of the Lord, according to all that his father Amaziah did." He imitated the good in his father's life, ignoring the bad, conduct worthy of emulation of sons today. Uzziah "sought God," but it was evidently due in large measure to the influence of the priest Zechariah, "who had understanding in the visions of God." In his desire to do that which

153

Jehovah required of him, the king, as many a man has since, found how helpful it is to turn at times to one who has close communion with the living God.

Prosperity of Righteousness.

And so we come to the first great lesson in Uzziah's long and eventful reign: " And as long as he sought the Lord, God made him to prosper."

It is no reflection on any man that his determination to do right is strengthened by a knowledge of the fact that God makes the righteous to prosper. The Bible abounds in declarations of the fact that the Heavenly Father has linked man's good with goodness.

The Psalmist announces, " Blessed is the man that walketh not in the counsel of the ungodly, nor standeth in the way of sinners, nor sitteth in the seat of the scornful." And again, " I have been young, and now am old; yet have I not seen the righteous forsaken, nor his seed begging bread." Solomon repeatedly points out the advantage of right doing. "For the upright shall dwell in the land, and the perfect shall remain in it," and " The blessing of the Lord, it maketh rich, and he addeth no sorrow with it."

Even collectively people prosper by doing right: " Righteousness exalteth a nation: but sin is a reproach to any people." Paul assures Timothy that " godliness is profitable unto all things." In Job we find that even Satan knew that there was a relation between prosperity and righteousness, although he regarded prosperity as an inducement to righteousness when it was a reward for righteousness. Christ gives us the Beatitudes, each one of which crowns virtue with reward.

It must not be understood, however, that the reward promised will necessarily be represented by dollars and cents. There are rewards immeasurably greater than money can buy; in fact, money itself is not always a blessing. Big fortunes in anticipation have ruined more young men than they have ever blest. An estate has often separated families after its enervating influence has sapped the strength of the children and made them a prey to luxury.

Other things being equal, righteousness brings a net result of good in any business or occupation.

A merchant may profit temporarily by dishonesty, but if he expects a prolonged success he must build upon a basis of fair dealing.

A lawyer may win a few cases by trickery, but in the long run, character, probity and truthfulness win out. The lawyer who deliberately tries to obscure the issue between right and wrong will finally find himself unable to discern the line when he looks for it, while the lawyer who conscientiously observes the oath which he takes to aid in the administration of justice and who endeavours to aid the judge and the jury in finding and applying the truth will increase his power to discern the truth, and thus become more valuable to his clients.

The Only Road to Real Success.

Even in politics (the word " even " is merely a concession to popular prejudice) it pays to be upright. Character is the power of endurance in man, and nowhere more than in politics.

But suppose that one could, by short cuts in business, in the professions, or in politics win more than he could by righteousness, " What shall it profit a man if he shall gain the whole world and lose his own soul? Or what shall a man give in exchange for his soul?"

Prosperity cannot be measured by the amount of food that one takes into his body, by the amount of clothing that one puts upon his back, or by the magnificence of the roof that shelters him. These things minister to the body. They are necessary, but the body is the least of man's possessions.

The possessions of the mind, though seemingly less necessary, are more precious than the things that supply man's physical wants, and the satisfactions of the soul are still greater and more lasting than the things that give mental pleasure.

Prosperity is the securing of that which is best for us, and righteousness is the only road that leads to real success.

Uzziah's Pride and Punishment.

The king sought the Lord in the days of his growth. "But when Uzziah was strong, his heart was lifted up to his destruction: for he transgressed against the Lord his God." Or, as the Revised Version has it, "His heart was lifted up, so that he did corruptly, and he transgressed against Jehovah his God."

His sin may seem trivial to those who put a light estimate upon the secret springs of action and the beginnings of evil. He "went into the temple of the Lord to burn incense upon the altar of incense." This was the duty of the priest. The king had no more authority in such matters than the caretaker of the Temple; he had no right to exercise priestly functions.

That he did not inadvertently sin is evident from the manner in which he resented the deserved rebuke. If the act had been due to ignorance, he would quickly have withdrawn when his attention was called to the law. But instead of that he resisted the four-score priests of Jehovah whom Azariah the chief priest called to his assistance. These defenders of the law withstood the king and said unto him, " It appertaineth not unto thee, Uzziah, to burn incense unto the Lord, but to the priests, the sons of Aaron, that are consecrated to burn incense."

But Uzziah was wroth and while he attempted to usurp the place of the priests " the leprosy even rose up in his forehead before the priests of the house of the Lord, from beside the incense altar." He recognised his punishment and made no further defense when he was thrust out of the temple; " yea, himself hasted also to go out because the Lord had smitten him."

God's Incomprehensible Laws.

Those who minimise the offense are apt to find fault with the punishment; because they think the sin relatively insignificant, they regard the punishment as relatively excessive. It is not necessary that man's finite mind shall comprehend God's laws in order to make them worthy of our respect and obedience.

Some who are prone to criticise the revealed will of God profess great reverence for God as He reveals Himself in nature. They charge God with cruelty if He visits a severe punishment upon those who disobey His revealed commandments and yet, they see about them in nature punishments more severe for acts which are due to ignorance or neglect. They see the careless paring of a toe nail cause death from blood poisoning; or exposure to the weather cause cold, followed by a fatal attack of pneumonia. They profess great respect for the lower forms of life and yet a few mosquitoes can depopulate a community by introducing yellow fever, and a few rats can spread a plague. Man is but a little lower than the angels and yet an invisible germ can usher him into eternity.

The Penalty of Pride.

The sin for which Uzziah was punished was one of the most common and, therefore, one that could not be overlooked—" Pride goeth before destruction, and an haughty spirit before a fall."

Pride suppresses sympathy by building artificial barriers between neighbours; pride has been the fruitful cause of war. In the case of Uzziah, it was a conspicuous sin in a conspicuous person. The evil example would have been greater than if the sin had been committed by one of the common people and the influence exerted by the punishment was likewise more salutary.

In Uzziah we see a very common type. He was virtuous until pride, inspired by success, brought about his downfall. It requires more moral strength to withstand great success than to endure the ordinary failures of life.

XXII

ISAIAH: THE PROCLAIMER OF PEACE

ISAIAH 2:2-4; 11:1-9

DO you long for world peace? Do you pray for it, strive for it? Would you know how world love and justice is to come?

Then turn to Isaiah. He was pre-eminently the prophet of peace, and in the two extracts from his great book which we shall consider today he brings his wonderful gift of imagery to bear upon this subject of supreme importance to the world.

The passages set down above are from the second and eleventh chapters. I shall take the liberty of transposing the quotations and refer to the second quotation first.

Isaiah speaks of the coming of the Messiah; He is to be of the seed of Abraham and a descendant of Jesse and David. "And the spirit of the Lord shall rest upon him, the spirit of wisdom and understanding, the spirit of counsel and might, the spirit of knowledge and of the fear of the Lord." The word "spirit" is here used four times and to this spirit is linked "the fear of the Lord."

We often hear the critics of the Bible finding fault with the word "fear." We are told that it is a narrow religion that teaches fear; that love should be a sufficient inducement to righteousness. Strange that the worshippers of Nature should overlook the fact that fear is written upon every page of Nature's book.

Fire is essential to human life, and yet we fear fire. We are afraid to thrust a hand into the fire or to allow fire to escape from man's control.

The air is necessary to life, and yet we fear the air when the wind rises to a certain velocity. The air in the form of a cyclone or hurricane is as destructive as fire unconfined.

And so with water. It is the daily need of every living thing, and yet it may take our lives when it comes in the form of a flood or we go into it beyond our depth.

Why not bring an indictment against Nature for exciting fear? Why should the very things that sustain life and give us the physical pleasures that we know become so deadly when their wrath is aroused?

The God of Nature is to be feared as well as loved— " the fear of the Lord is the beginning of wisdom." Only the foolish find fault with fear as a restraining agency. The fear of God holds us in check until we reach a point where our " delight is in the law of the Lord."

Isaiah has the Messiah delighting " in the fear of the Lord." Obedience comes before the knowledge; the child learns to obey before it knows the reason why. Is not the difference between man and the Heavenly Father as great as the difference between the parent and the child?

" A Little Child Shall Lead Them."

The coming Messiah was not to be dependent upon the avenues of information upon which ordinary mortals have to rely. A human judge learns by sight and by ear, but the Messiah could not be dependent upon seeming things. " He shall not judge after the sight of

his eyes, neither reprove after the hearing of his ears."
He would have an insight into the truth, even the spirit
of wisdom, and of understanding and of knowledge.
He would judge the poor with righteousness and " reprove with equity for the meek of the earth."

Throughout history the righteous judge has been
described as the one who does justice to the poor. It
was one of the proofs that Christ gave of His Messiah-
ship—" the poor have the gospel preached to them."

The prophet's description of the completeness of the
peace that was to come leaves nothing to be imagined.
Even the animals are to be purged of the savagery that
dominates their world.   " The wolf also shall dwell
with the lamb and the leopard shall lie down with the
kid; and the calf and the young lion and the fatling
together; and a little child shall lead them "—one of
the wonderful sentences that Isaiah coined for the
world.

Probably no one save Christ has ever so exalted the
child, although throughout the ages child leadership has
been an outstanding fact. A child's tiny hands, before
they can lift a featherweight, bring two hearts nearer
together, and its presence sobers the thoughtless and
makes them begin to plan for life a real thing. Many
a drinking man, when asked why he voted against the
saloon, has answered: " I have a son," and the answer
is sufficient. The child educates the parent while the
parent instructs the child.

The Blessings of Peace.

Isaiah puts the Messiah upon a world throne. " He
shall judge among the nations, and shall rebuke many
people." Then follows the oft-quoted picture of peace
universal and perpetual: " And they shall beat their

swords into plowshares, and their spears into pruning-hooks; nation shall not lift up sword against nation, neither shall they learn war any more."

Dr. Jowett calls attention to the fact that reform does not cause a diminution of energy, but rather a diversion of energy from destruction to construction. The metal in the swords is valuable; it is not to be consigned to the waste pile, but to be employed for the benefit of mankind. The plowshare is the symbol of the labour of the agriculturist, just as the pruning-hook represents the tools of the orchard. There will be more food when there is less war—the blessings of peace will be more satisfying than the triumphs of the battlefield.

We are often asked what substitute will be found for war; what will stir man to heroic deeds? There are some who go so far as to argue that man is so slothful and indolent that nothing less than fear of immediate death will bring forth a maximum effort, as if man would degenerate without an occasional opportunity to shed his brother's blood!

Rivalries in Helpful Service.

No warrant for such a base philosophy can be found in history, sacred or profane. If killing were necessary for man's highest development, governments would make provision for it. We would have commissions empowered to examine men and permit a return to savagery whenever it was necessary to insure civilisa-tion. But instead of that we have a law against murder among all people and under all governments.

When the hatred that leads to war is banished, love will lead to rivalries in helpful service to mankind.

In passing, it may be proper to notice that there is a

school or group of learned men who argue that war is necessary to prevent overcrowding. Beginning with Malthus, these so-called philosophers have calculated on the awful consequences that will follow if the world is not depopulated from time to time by the slaughter of the battlefield.

Generally speaking, economists can be divided in two classes: those who try to increase the supply of food to meet human needs, and those who try to restrict the population to fit the food. Fortunately the first group is in the majority of civilised society, while the members of the second group find few who are willing to adopt their brutish plan or even listen to their senseless predictions.

"The Prince of Peace."

It is to Isaiah that we are indebted for one of the most striking descriptive names bestowed upon the Saviour—He shall be called (this is but one of His titles) "the Prince of Peace." The next verse of chapter nine is not quoted as frequently as verse six, but it contains a prophecy that explains and justifies the title given to Christ: " Of the increase of his government and peace there shall be no end." Few verses in the Old Testament contain so much of hope for the world as do these found in the book of the prophet Isaiah.

There is a gloomy philosophy that teaches that all governments must necessarily die. We are told that a government, like an individual, has its birth, its youth, its maturity, and then, like an individual, must decline and die.

Comparisons are only valuable when they are truthful; they may be, and are, very deceptive when they are false. This is one of the many false comparisons that have found currency.

While the government is, each day, in control of the people then living, it is, in a much larger sense, composed of generations rather than of individuals. Its life is continuous; as one generation passes off the stage another comes on. As there is no break in the chain of generations there is no necessary reason why a future government should be weaker or worse than the present, unless there is some necessary reason why future generations should be weaker or worse than the present.

Christ Alone Can Bring Peace.

Isaiah encourages the optimist when he announces that the government and peace of the coming Messiah, our Christ, will increase without end. Isaiah also gives the reason in the same verse: It will be established " with judgment and with justice from henceforth even for ever."

If Christ is to the world what His followers believe Him to be, He is to redeem man from sin and then guide him in the paths of righteousness that lead to peace.

If one will but examine the fabric of civilisation, he will find that all its strongest threads and brightest colours came from the teachings of Christ. His Golden Rule is the only one that can make business honest; His doctrine of forgiveness is the only rule that can save man from the corroding influence of the spirit of revenge; the love that He taught is the only weapon for which there is no shield.

Christ's philosophy fits into every human need; His moral code, and it alone, can solve the problems that vex the heart and perplex the world.

XXIII

HEZEKIAH: THE REPENTANT RULER

II Chronicles 30: 1-9, 13

A VERY pleasing picture and a much-needed lesson for today—that is what you will find if you turn to the thirteenth chapter of Second Chronicles.

Hezekiah, the good king of Judah, about whom the Old Testament historian writes in this passage, deserves to be counted among the idealists, and there is a fascination about his vision of a reunited race, as set forth by the ancient chronicler.

He longed to see the kingdoms of Israel and Judah one—they had been separated for two hundred and fifty years—and he chose the only way of bringing them together, namely, a revival of their interest in the one God whom the two factions worshipped. He sent to all Israel and Judah and wrote letters to the half tribes of Ephraim and Manasseh inviting them to come to the house of God at Jerusalem and keep the Passover unto the Lord God of Israel.

The Passover, the great feast of the Jews, had not been observed in latter years as it had been in the earlier, and, with disregard for the things held in common, came increasing enmity between the two segments of the Hebrew people.

From " Dan to Beersheba," or from " Beersheba to Dan," a phrase used to include the entire land from north to south, the proclamation was carried by runners and great preparations were made for the feast.

Hezekiah not only admitted the sins of the fathers, but he used their sins to stimulate a new spirit of faith and worship. While he pleaded with the people to return to the God of their fathers, he called attention to the punishment visited upon those guilty of apostasy: "God gave them up to desolation, as ye see."

The Simple Remedy.

Hezekiah's remedy was very simple. "Yield yourself unto the Lord, and enter into his sanctuary, which he hath sanctified for ever: and serve the Lord your God." Here are the three steps necessary.

Surrender of self comes first. Their fathers had been "stiff-necked," a term used to describe habitual resistance to God's appeal. No use for them to enter the sanctuary until the spirit of rebellion gave way to the spirit of reverence.

Is there anything unreasonable in such a requirement? The Commandments begin with, "Thou shalt have no other gods before me." This implies surrender to the Heavenly Father. God must have the first place; even self, the false god that has the largest number of worshippers, must be put aside that Jehovah may have the supreme place.

Christ reiterated this requirement when He condensed into one the commandments that relate to man's duty to God and proclaimed as the first and great commandment, "Thou shalt love the Lord thy God with all thy heart, and with all thy soul, and with all thy mind."

The entering of the sanctuary naturally followed surrender to God.

As long as one is insurgent against his Creator, he does not feel at home among the obedient. Just as soon as the proper relationship is established between man and his Maker, he finds it easy to be a co-worker with worshippers like himself. Love of neighbour follows closely after love of God. That is the natural order, and because it is the natural order the brotherhood of man is not to be expected until the Fatherhood of God is acknowledged.

When one surrenders himself to God and unites with his brethren, service is not only natural but necessary. The thought of service does not come to one who is not one with God or to one who is out of sympathy with those about him; it comes with love of God and fellowship with other Christians—an atmosphere in which indolence is impossible.

The Promise of Reward.

Hezekiah holds out the promise of reward if the children of Israel will do their part: " Serve the Lord your God, that the fierceness of His wrath may turn away from you." Even the heart of their oppressors will be softened; if the people show their fidelity to God, they shall find compassion before their captors and be permitted to return to their own land. Hezekiah gives us a conception of God that history has justified: God is gracious and merciful, and will not turn away His face from those who return to Him.

We are told that there were assembled at Jerusalem much people—a very great assembly—to keep the feast of unleavened bread. Hezekiah did not accomplish all that he had hoped for. Some scoffed at him and ridiculed his efforts, but many found in the Passover an opportunity for reconciliation.

The world today has to meet the problem that confronted the children of Israel, and Hezekiah's plan commends itself to those who are interested in uniting the religious forces of the world to combat the materialistic influences that would rob life of its spiritual element. All the metals fuse at some heat; nothing but heat can unite them. Today, the religious world is divided into many factions, and antagonism between various factions prevents cooperation even in matters about which they agree. Christian and Jew, Protestant and Catholic unite on a number of fundamentals, but they too often emphasise the differences instead of the points upon which they agree.

The Duty of All Creeds.

To illustrate: All believe in God—this is the basis of their religious faith. One cannot claim a greater devotion than the other to the Heavenly Father whom they worship as all loving, all wise, and all powerful. They equally revere Him as the source of religious sentiment and as the object of adoration. All acknowledge a sense of responsibility to God for thought and word and deed. This sense of responsibility is the most potent influence that acts upon a life.

All believe in prayer; no group will concede that any other is more sincere or constant in expressions of gratitude to God or in petitions for God's guidance.

All believe in a future life where we shall have to render an account of the deeds done in the flesh.

All believe in the coming of universal brotherhood,

which is the manward expression of faith in the Fatherhood of God.

Here are four vital elements in the life that rests upon a belief in God.

Back to God!

Just now the world is suffering from the ignoring of God's law of rewards. Every human being must draw every day from the sum of human toil. Many are not only ignorant of, but indifferent to, the basis of rewards. Instead of asking, How much can I rightfully draw from society? they inquire how much they can secure and by what means they can secure it. Their thought is not centered upon earning power, but upon power to absorb without regard to ethics or equity.

The first step toward the establishment on earth of God's law of rewards is to restore faith in God as a real personality—as a living God whose love purposes all things, whose wisdom plans all things, and whose power is able to enforce His purposes; and take away a belief in God and you destroy consciousness of responsibility, prayer, belief in immortality, and the tie of kinship that binds each to every other. All believers in God who believe in moral responsibility to God, petitions to Jehovah, hope of heaven, and brotherhood, must be equally interested in guarding from attack belief in God as the one foundation stone. If religion had a spokesman who stood before the divided and estranged worshippers of God as Hezekiah stood before his own divided race, his call would be framed in the same spirit and in much the same language as Hezekiah employed. Back to God! is still the plea that is necessary. Back to God, who is just in His judgment and immeasurable in His love and mercy.

Those who differ in their applications of religion to life can be brought together only by so intensifying faith in God and reverence for Him as to dissolve their differences in a unity of purpose and of faith. " By their fruits ye shall know them "; that form or religion —that interpretation of God—is nearest to the truth which brings man most humbly and completely into subjection to God's will and makes him most earnest and most constant in seeking guidance each day.

A return to a whole-hearted, whole-souled, whole-minded belief in God must now, as in the past, be the hope of those who would be true to the heavenly vision.

XXIV

HILKIAH: THE RE-DISCOVERER OF THE LAW

II CHRONICLES 34: 14-16, 29-32

THIS is the age of discovery. Archæologists, inventors, chemists, astronomers are continually bringing forth new wonders for us to contemplate. Within the span of a few years we have been given the automobile, the flying machine, the submarine, the wireless telegraph, the radio-telephone, and from ugly and apparently useless substances come forth, under the magic touch of the chemist, wondrous colours to make brilliant the garments of the world and medicines to heal the sick. Discovery is piled upon discovery in such rapidity that oftentimes we are bewildered thereby.

But, wonderful and far-reaching in their effects on life as these discoveries are, you will have to turn to the thirty-fourth chapter of Second Chronicles to learn of what is still, and always will remain, one of the greatest discoveries in history; for twenty-five hundred years ago, in the reign of Josiah, king of Judah, the Bible, that had been lost, was found—the " book of the law of the Lord given by Moses."

Just how and for how long the Book that has shaped the destiny of the world was lost is not definitely known, but the fact that in the course of the history of the Jewish kingdom it was lost is proof that it was neglected. If it had been in daily use, if the people had shaped their lives according to its precepts, its disappearance would have been at once noted and its recovery soon announced. But the Jews were led by rulers who oscillated from fidelity to God to subservience to heathen gods, and the punishment that follows wrongdoing carried many of them captive into foreign lands. And some time during these black years the "book of the law of the Lord given by Moses," the Bible, was lost.

An Example of Early Piety.

It was during this dismal time in the history of the Jews that Josiah, who was the son of a wicked father, began his reign in Jerusalem at eight years of age; when he was only ten he sought after "the God of David." He is one of the many illustrations in the Bible of early piety. We are not informed as to the influences that moulded him, but as he could not have been the pupil of his father the honour falls to his mother, Jedidah, or to some of the priestly class.

Before taking up his work that led to the Bible's recovery, it may be well to observe that a large percentage of those who enter upon a Christian life begin young. There are several reasons for this.

First, the environment of a Christian home creates conditions in which faith germinates. The child, sooner than many suppose, finds its heart taking hold upon faith in God and in Christ.

Faith is a much earlier growth than reason. According to law, the young man is presumed to be immature in his reason until he is twenty-one. No evidence of precocity can overthrow this presumption. The calendar is the only proof that the courts will receive. Until a boy is twenty-one his deed is not valid and his vote is not received. While maturity in woman is presumed to arrive a little earlier than in man, it, too, is calculated by years; differences that manifest themselves in individuals are not taken into consideration.

With faith it is different. Faith in the parent springs up early in the child and this faith naturally broadens into faith in others until the child, long before it reaches legal maturity, can worship God and give its love to Christ in return for Christ's love.

The Period of Rebellion.

The second reason is to be found in the fact that every child passes through a period of rebellion, latent or expressed, against parental authority. The Prodigal Son gives us an exhibition of this rebellion carried to the point of separation from home.

In most cases affection, if not wisdom, restrains the child during the years when youth is passing into maturity. This is essentially true if, before this transition period comes, the child has learned to supplement the authority of the parent with the authority of a loving Heavenly Father. Obedience to parents makes obedience to God easier, and obedience to God strengthens the child's respect for its parents.

The peril of the child is increased by the fact that just at the time when the spirit of independence is taking the place of parental authority he begins to study the universe about him.

At this period any theory that relieves the child of a sense of responsibility is more attractive than it is earlier or later, and, therefore, many are led away from faith in God. Some afterward return as intellectual prodigal sons; some wander off into a starless night even though they recognise, as Romanes did, the awful

contrast between the "hallowed creed" of their youth
and "the lonely mystery of existence" as they find it
to be when they abandon belief in God.

Fortunate for the child if its religious faith becomes
firmly rooted before it encounters the strong temptations that come as it approaches manhood or womanhood. No one who has come in contact with ship-
wrecked lives will take the responsibility of advising a
child to postpone a confession of its faith when its
heart is ready to make a confession.

Hilkiah Finds the Book.

At the age of twenty Josiah began to purge his
country of every form of idolatry that had become rife
throughout its borders during the brief reign of his
wicked father and the long reign of his grandfather;
at twenty-six he began to repair Solomon's Temple,
that had been allowed to fall into decay while the
idolatrous held their revels and orgies and human sacri-
fices. It was at this time that Hilkiah, the high priest,
unearthed the lost word of God, what is supposed to
have been the Pentateuch.

When the book was brought to the king there was
great rejoicing. He gathered together all the elders of
Judah and Jerusalem and then he brought to the house
of the Lord all the inhabitants, the priests and the
people. Standing in his place, he read to them "all
the words of the book of the covenant that was found
in the house of the Lord"; and he made a covenant
before the Lord to walk after the Lord and to keep his
commandments and his testimonies and his statutes
with all his heart, and with all his soul" to perform the
words of the covenant that were written in the book.

He not only made a promise for himself, but he

brought his people into the covenant with him, and they " did according to the covenant of God, the God of their fathers."

Several of those who write upon the lessons that the Bible teaches have found in this account of the loss and recovery of the Bible a suggestion as to the numerous ways in which the Word of God is lost now, for it goes without saying that an individual, as well as a nation, may lose the Bible, and lose it today as well as in the past.

The reason is not the same in all cases; anything that is substituted for the Bible will serve to banish it from the thought. If one obeys the first commandment, " Thou shalt have no other gods before me," he will be anxious to keep in touch with God's word and will want to know God's will that he may obey it. If he worships any of the many false gods, he will feel little interest in the Word of God. In fact, he will deliberately avoid it because its language will accuse him.

The False Gods of Today.

It is hardly necessary to say that there are as many false gods today as there were in the days of the Hebrew kings, or that the temptation to worship these gods is as strong today as then.

We have the god of gold, worshipped by those who put money above everything else; the god of fashion, worshipped by those who long for distinction in the social world; the god of fame, before which those prostrate themselves who set their heart upon the distinctions that can be won in any department of activity.

We have the god of ease, which those worship who think only of food and bodily comfort—and the satisfying of physical appetites.

We have the god of intellect, worshipped by those who, putting the brain above the heart, and reason above faith, proudly follow the wanderings of the mind instead of humbly trusting the Word of God.

We have the travel god, worshipped by those who develop the wanderlust and associate with rare and unusual things until the little tasks that make up everyday life pall upon them.

We have the god of chance, worshipped by those who are bent on getting something for nothing; the god of passion, worshipped by those who subordinate the mind and the soul to the gratification of the body; the rum god, in whose worship Americans used to spend more than on education and religion combined; and, last and most deceptive of all, the great god self, of which all the other false gods are but masks.

The Great God Self.

It is self that obscures the Creator—self that is puffed up with its own importance and seeks to make the world subservient to it; self that could not live an hour if it had to give its attention to its own vital organs. One would die of exhaustion if he had to swing the pendulum of the heart or pump the bellows of the lungs or direct the digestive organs in their unceasing work.

But the Heavenly Father has provided that man can live without conscious effort in order that man may devote his thought to God's work and to the welfare of his fellows. And yet, many give to their Maker no thought at all and are indifferent to His revealed word.

Josiah, twenty-five hundred years ago, recognised the value of God's word and led the people in the making of a covenant for the worship of Jehovah. He entered into these covenants with "all his heart and with all his soul." If Josiah and his people so highly prized the Pentateuch, what should be our estimate of the Bible as we have it—the Old Testament enlarged and a New Testament added?

What the Bible Gives Us.

I venture to say that the Bible has done more to determine the civilisation of today than all other books combined.

It gives the conception of God entertained by the civilised world; it gives us an infallible guide—a lamp unto our feet and a light unto our path.

It gives us the only authentic account of Christ, whose life on earth began with a virgin birth and ended in a resurrection—the greatest fact of history and the growing figure of all time.

The world never needed the Bible more than now; it needs a personal God, near enough to hear prayer and willing to answer; it needs an inspired Word of God; it needs the full-statured Christ of whom the Bible tells.

XXV

JEREMIAH: THE FEARLESS

JEREMIAH 26: 8-16

WE have been thrilled by the words and soul-stirring experiences of Elijah, Elisha and Isaiah. We come now to one who shares with them the reverence bestowed by the children of Israel upon the great " men of God."

Jeremiah was the son of Hilkiah, probably that Hilkiah, the high priest, who, in the reign of King Josiah of Judah, found the book of the law of God in the temple in Jerusalem after it had been lost through long idolatrous years and thus restored the Bible to the world.

He was also a relative of Huldah, the prophetess. He was brought up among the priests and officiated in the temple. He was unmarried, being, by God's command, kept free from family obligations that he might devote his entire time and strength to his prophetic work.

Jeremiah's Heavy Task.

Jeremiah was designated for the Lord's work before he was born and was called when he was quite young. In his modesty he protested, " I cannot speak, for I am a child." The Lord replied that he should speak whatever Jehovah commanded and that he should not be afraid, for God promised to deliver him and put words in his mouth.

Then his work was outlined: " See, I have this day set thee over the nations and over the kingdoms, to root out, and to pull down, and to destroy, and to throw down, to build and to plant."

It was not a pleasant task to which Jeremiah was assigned. To be " set over the nations and over the kingdoms, to root out and to pull down, and to destroy " would necessarily arouse antagonism and create strife. But Jeremiah was to do more than that; he was " to build, and to plant "—much more enjoyable work than merely pulling down.

Our study has to do with the work of the prophet after the death of Judah's good King Josiah, he who cleansed the kingdom of idolatry and restored Solomon's temple, turning the nation once again back to the living God.

Jehoiakim departed from the ways of his father and his conduct stirred the heart of the great Jeremiah, who was commissioned by the Almighty to make a final appeal to the king and to warn him and his people that the Temple would become " like Shiloh " and Jerusalem, " a curse to all the nations of the earth." Shiloh, the ancient religious capital of the Jews, had become a ruin, and its very name was a reproach.

An Example of Superb Courage.

The warning, uttered with all the earnestness of Jeremiah's nature, aroused the priests, the prophets and the people to a frenzy. They seized him and said, " Thou shalt surely die."

It was a perilous thing to speak for God among a people who had turned away from Him. They invoked the form of the law after having disregarded its spirit. It was the duty of the prophet to convey to the

people any message which God communicated to him,
but the authorities thought it was a thing worthy of
death to prophesy against the city as Jeremiah had done.

Here we have the boldness that becomes the man
who is the spokesman of God. Standing unafraid
before his accusers, he is indifferent as to himself. " I
am in your hand; do with me as seemeth good and
meet unto you."

Jeremiah was less concerned about his own safety
than he was about the fate of Jerusalem and his people.
Whether they shed his blood or not meant little to him,
but to bring innocent blood upon themselves and upon
the city was a matter of greater moment. " But know
ye for certain that if ye put me to death ye shall bring
innocent blood upon yourselves and upon this city."
God had sent him to speak His message and had warned
him, " Diminish not a word," and he performed his
duty faithfully.

No Excuse for Duty Neglected.

The result was what it usually is. It is hard for
even the wicked to resist the courage of an earnest man.
If Jeremiah had shown weakness or betrayed fear, his
life would no doubt have paid the penalty. But when
he faced them, willing to suffer death, but unwilling to
be disloyal to God or unfaithful to his fellow-men, he
triumphed over his enemies. " Then said the princes
and all the people unto the priests and to the prophets:
' This man is not worthy to die: for he hath spoken
unto us in the name of the Lord our God.' "

The application of the lesson is very plain. There
can be no evasion of duty. One can waive his rights—
it is sometimes wise to do so, but there is no excuse
that any one can give for failure to perform a duty.

In the olden days God called men by a voice that was audible or through an agent who was visible; today the call is often as unmistakable, even though the ear hears not the message and though the messenger may not be seen. We have the prayer route between God's children and the Father's throne. We can seek guidance and we can feel a spiritual urge to the doing of the things that should be done. The heart that is open to divine suggestion will be led aright—" Seek, and ye shall find; knock, and it shall be opened unto you."

There is no doubt as to God's doing His part; the only question is, will man be faithful? Will those who have convictions, founded upon an understanding of God's Word and on answers to sincere appeals for guidance, have the courage to speak out and proclaim the truth revealed unto them, or will they fear for themselves and remain silent?

The Only Way to Better Things.

Jeremiah is a great example of fearless proclamation of truth regardless of personal consequences. He points the way to reform and no new way has been discovered. All great moral movements have started with a Jeremiah who dared to proclaim truth as it was revealed to him. The Jeremiahs are the pivots upon which history turns.

Truth is not born in the crowd; its appearance is not greeted with applause. Truth is born in solitude—in travail that often costs the life of the one who gives it birth. But what matters it what becomes of the man who proclaims it if the truth itself be safely launched upon the world? The prophet may be like " a voice crying in the wilderness," but the voice echoes and echoes and echoes until it drowns out all other sounds.

In the willingness of man to die for the truth we find conclusive proof that man was made in the image of God. Martyr blood does not come from a brute lineage. This unconcern about self, this devotion to things greater than self, is the most God-like thing in man.

The growth of truth may be difficult to explain, but it is natural; we see it about us every day. Some one has said: "You may build your capitols until they reach the skies, but if they rest upon injustice the pulse of woman will beat them down." The pulse is the symbol of life, and because there is life in truth it demolishes error, however strongly error may seem to be entrenched. Of Truth it has been said: "The eternal years of God are hers."

Jeremiahs Always Needed.

We have frequent proof, too, that merely from the standpoint of personal safety, courage is better than cowardice. Many a man has purchased his life by seeming indifference to death, while others have invited violence by showing fear.

As "darkness brings out the stars," so the evil days that come to a community, to a state, to a nation or to the world bring out some one with the voice of warning which, if heeded, restores righteousness and with it peace and prosperity. Where the voice is unheeded we learn anew that "the wages of sin is death."

Every generation needs Jeremiahs whose convictions are deep enough to override all the restraints of caution and so-called prudence. They may be unpopular with evildoers, but they are necessary for the establishment of truth and virtue and justice.

XXVI

EHOAIKIM: THE WHITTLER OF THE WORD

JEREMIAH 36: 4-8, 20-24, 32

THE Rev. Perry Wayland Sinks has written a little book which suggests a title for this chapter, namely, *"Whittlers of the Word."* He takes as his text part of our text—the twenty-third verse of the dramatic thirty-sixth chapter of Jeremiah, which describes Jehoiakim, king of Judah, cutting the roll, or book, of the word of God with his penknife, and casting it into the fire in the brazier before him, until all the word of the Lord was consumed.

It is an appropriate text for the present day.

In the first year of king Jehoiakim's reign, the great prophet, Jeremiah, had stood up boldly for God in His house, exhorting the people to turn back to the God of their fathers, and false priests and false prophets and the people themselves, given over to idolatry, had cried out for his death. Now, after four years of equally zealous and courageous exhortation in the name of the living God, Jeremiah was "shut up" and could not go into the house of the Lord, in Jerusalem.

We are not informed as to the character of the restraints placed upon him. It did not seem to be an imprisonment, and he may have been kept at home (or merely excluded from the Temple) by order of the king because of the indignation caused by his outspoken condemnation of the conduct of the king and those who joined with him in the repudiation of God's leadership.

The King Destroys the Word.

At any rate, the prophet betook himself to writing. If he were not permitted to go into the temple and there proclaim the warnings given him of the Lord, then he would do the next best thing, namely, commit them to writing and have a messenger read them. This he did, selecting Baruch as his amanuensis and spokesman. He chose the fast day as one that would be most likely to bring a crowd into the temple. Possibly he may have thought, too, that on such a day the people would be more sensitive to religion and more willing to listen to one who spoke in the name of the Almighty. Baruch followed the instructions given by Jeremiah and read in the book the words of the Lord in the Lord's house.

As might have been expected, news of Jeremiah's bold deed was at once carried to the king and he sent Jehudi to fetch the roll. There in the winter house, or the winter part of the palace, with the princes about him, the king heard the warnings of the prophet. A fire was burning in the brazier before him and into this fire he threw the roll, three or four leaves at a time, which he cut out with his penknife as they were read.

The Penknife of Criticism.

The next verse tells us that neither the king nor any of his servants were afraid; they did not rend their garments nor give any of the customary evidences of grief or regret over the sacrilegious act.

If Jeremiah were living today he would not have to

change the wording of the text materially to describe the work of the destructive critics as they cut the Bible into pieces with the penknife of criticism and cast the fragments into the fire.

Whether they are actuated by the same motive that led Jehoiakim to mutilate and burn the roll containing the warnings which the Lord uttered through Jeremiah cannot be known without an inquiry into their own lives. They may have some of the pride that made Jehoiakim take offense at a reminder of his sins and of the punishment with which the Lord threatened him.

These critics repudiate the account of the fall of man as indignantly as the wicked Judæan king repudiated Jeremiah's description of the fall of Israel and are as indifferent to the means by which man is to be restored as Jehoiakim was to the plan offered for the restoration of Israel.

These "whittlers of the Word" begin at the first chapter of Genesis and employ their penknives on the Mosaic account of man's creation. This, they say, cannot be true because man is merely a descendant of the brute.

Attacks on the Bible's Veracity.

Even if this doctrine did not affect man's philosophy of life, such an hypothesis ought not to be accepted without proof because of the attack it makes upon the veracity of the Scriptures. As the Bible has but one central thought, namely, man in his relation to God, an indictment of the Bible's account of man's creation, if proven, weakens the foundation upon which confidence in the Bible rests.

But when it is seen that the overthrow of the Bible

account of man's creation changes the whole philosophy of life, one understands how important it is to demand proof before conceding the evolutionary hypothesis.

If man is placed upon the earth for a purpose, created by special act of God and made a part of the Maker's plan, his highest duty, as it should be his greatest pleasure, is to learn God's will concerning him and to do it. If, on the contrary, he is a blood-relative of the animals of the field and of the beasts of the forest, duty cannot be an imperative word to him.

If he is the child of the Almighty, made in the Father's image, he cannot escape a sense of responsibility for thought, word, and deed. If, on the contrary, his family tree is as Darwin outlines it and he must count every form of life as ancestry or collateral relatives, he can scarcely feel that he is accountable for anything that he does.

A sense of responsibility, when strained through the blood of fish, reptile, bird and beast, loses its power to bind that which we know as conscience, if with such an ancestry man can claim to have a conscience.

Robbing Christ of His Glory.

But the harm done by the critics is not confined to the destruction of reverence for God and the weakening of the desire to please Him; the reasons that lead to the rejection of the Bible account of man's creation lead logically to the rejection of everything else in the Bible that distinguishes it from writings of uninspired men.

Darwinism eliminates all the miraculous. The miracle is inconsistent with evolution; for this reason one of the prominent leaders of evolution has recently tried to annihilate all the miracles with an alliteration. He says, " Miracles are scientifically improbable, historically unreliable, practically undesirable, and, therefore, unbelievable." Any hypothesis that will make " unbelievable " the record of man's creation in the image of God will exclude all the miracles contained in the Old and New Testaments.

When all miracles are excluded, Christ is robbed of the glory of His virgin birth, of the majesty of His deity and of the triumph of His resurrection.

The same logic that excludes miracles excludes also the supernatural. In his comment on the verses that give us our text, a higher critic says, " Jeremiah was one of the great prophetic souls who walked so close to God that he recognised in every conviction that came to him the promptings of the divine voice. Accordingly, etc." Here the stiletto is deftly inserted in the heart of the prophecies. According to this critic, Jeremiah did not receive any direct communications from God, as the prophet says he did, but simply had " convictions " which he recognised as " promptings of the divine voice." The same logic removes every evidence of the supernatural to be found in the Testaments, Old and New.

When the Whittlers Get Through.

When the " whittlers of the Word " get through with the Bible it is not quite as good as a book of fiction because, if the indictment is true, it has to bear the odium of having pretended to be what it is not. The Bible is the basis of the Christian religion. If the Creator, instead of being a personal God, is so far away that man can have no consciousness of His presence in daily life, so far away that He cannot hear or answer prayer, He is little if any better than the No-God of the materialists.

If the Bible, instead of being an inspired book and an infallible guide to our feet, is just a collection of sayings of men, it has no more authority than any other book.

If Christ, instead of being the Son of God and Saviour of the world, sent to redeem man by His blood and to guide him by His example, was just a deluded enthusiast, if not a designing impostor, He cannot be of any great consequence to society.

When Jehoiakim destroyed the roll of the words of the Lord as received by Jeremiah, he did not substitute anything for it; he destroyed but he did not create. So with the critics of the Bible; they play the part of Iago —they whisper suspicions and damning insinuations.

They root up faith in the minds of the young and tear down religious belief, but they offer nothing in place of that which they destroy.

They cannot save man from the voyage upon the sea of life, but they remove the moral rudder that must guide his ship if it is to reach the haven in safety, and then they mockingly bid him bon voyage as he ventures forth without chart or compass.

An Impregnable Rock.

The closing verse of our text tells us that Jeremiah took another roll and, giving it to Baruch the scribe, dictated to him all the words of the book that Jehoiakim had burned in the fire and added to them many like words. The wicked king could burn the parchment on which the words of the Lord, as given to the prophet, were written, but he was powerless to destroy the prophecies or to prevent their fulfillment.

And so, today, the critics may mutilate the Bible passages to which they take exceptions, but they are powerless to destroy the Christian religion, to which the Bible has given birth.

The impregnable rock of Holy Scripture still stands and will stand. They cannot rob God of His omnipotence or of His nearness; they cannot rob the revealed Word of God of its truth; they cannot rob Christ of His power to save those who put their trust in Him.

XXVII

ZEDEKIAH: THE DISRUPTER OF JUDAH

II Kings 25: 1-12

HOW graphically the closing days of the kingdom of Judah makes plain the inexorable working of this great moral law: "Be not deceived; God is not mocked: for whatsoever a man soweth, that shall he also reap."

Again and again, as kings came and went, the people of Jerusalem had scorned the prophets, turned to idolatrous practices, steeped themselves in the vices and sins of the heathen nations round about them, forgotten and mocked God. And now the harvest.

But even as the people of Jerusalem looked out over the city's walls upon the besieging host brought against them by the mighty king Nebuchadnezzar of Babylon, God gave them their last chance to avert the terrible harvest of their own sowing. Through Jeremiah the prophet He had counseled: "Desist in your rebellion against your overlord, surrender to the Chaldeans, repent of your sins, and Jerusalem will not be destroyed and you shall live." But the stiff-necked rulers of Judah preferred their own judgment to the guidance of the Almighty, and, hence, national disaster complete and full followed.

Proof of Progress.

From the ninth unto the eleventh year of king Zedekiah's reign, Nebuchadnezzar besieged Jerusalem round

about. Then the city's food supply gave out, famine
fell upon the people, a breach was made in the walls,
and all Zedekiah's men of war and the king himself
fled by night from the might and wrath of the Chaldean
host. But the enemy pursued and overtook the Hebrew
king in the plains of Jericho, made him prisoner, scattered his army from him, and took him up to Nebuchadnezzar to the town of Riblah for judgment.

What followed when the two kings came face to
face is proof that the world has made some progress
even in war.

While the purpose of war has not changed; while
the taking of human life is still the first aim of war,
and while outrages are still practiced by soldiers in the
heat of passion and under the impulse of revenge, no
civilised government would be guilty of the cruelties
that were openly practiced in olden times. The Chaldeans slew the sons of the captive king before his eyes,
and then they put out the eyes of the king himself.
Any government that would now thus torture a prisoner, helpless in that government's hands, would call
down upon itself the condemnation of the world.

But in the time of which we write the slaughtering
of conquered people was not an uncommon thing.
That was a part of war whenever it did its bloody
work, and the torture of Zedekiah was not out of har-
mony with cruelties then practiced.

Destruction of Jerusalem.

Nor was it an uncommon thing to destroy a conquered city. And so Nebuzar-adan, a captain of the
guard in the Chaldean army, was sent to Jerusalem to
destroy it.

He did his work effectively. He burned the house

of the Lord, and the king's house, and every great
man's house in the city. The walls were broken down,
and the inhabitants who were left, except the poorest,
were carried away captive to Babylon. But the poor
of the land were left to care for the vineyards and the
farms. Thus Jerusalem was left desolate, its fate
being just what Jeremiah, speaking by divine inspiration, had foretold. God made him His messenger to
the people, but they would not believe, and their punishment followed.

The most striking part of the Biblical description of
Nebuzar-adan's desolating work relates to the destruction of Solomon's temple.

In beauty it was one of the wonders of the world.
Its cost has been estimated at from two and a half to
four billion dollars—an appalling sum even now and
relatively much greater then.

Thirty thousand men were employed in cutting the
cedar that was brought from Lebanon for the temple.
The masons and others who aided in its construction
were numbered at 150,000. When it is remembered
that the building was not remarkable for its size
(ninety feet long, thirty feet wide and forty-five feet
high), the outlay upon ornamentation must have
been vast.

Looting of the Temple.

" And the pillars of brass that were in the house of
the Lord, and the bases, and the brasen sea that were
in the house of the Lord, did the Chaldeans break in
pieces, and carried the brass of them to Babylon. And
the pots and the shovels and the snuffers and spoons
and other vessels of brass, and the firepan, the bowls
and such things as were of gold, in gold, and of silver,

in silver," were likewise carried away. The looting of the Temple left no treasure overlooked.

While the historical facts are of very great interest, the lessons that the facts teach are of still greater value to us. We are prone to exaggerate the visible and to underestimate the invisible—prone also to be more shocked at the destruction of valuable property than at the disobedience that imperils everything.

What a place Jerusalem would be for tourists if Solomon's Temple were still there!

When I visited the Holy City I was surprised to learn that but a small fraction of the tourists who go to Egypt are interested in the Holy Land. Not many thousands turn aside to visit the soil made sacred by the tread of the prophets and by the blood of the Saviour. It is a land of relics and of ruins. A few Jews wail by the walls of the Temple and a few pilgrims wander from place to place in search of the hallowed spots described in the Bible. There is controversy about nearly every point of interest, so that one is seldom sure that he is seeing the places that he came to see. If the Temple of Solomon were only there in all its beauty and magnificence, the lovers of art would wend their way to it from every land.

The Only Stable Foundation.

Christ made impressive use of the difference between the house built upon the rock and the house built upon the sand. Solomon's Temple was a religious structure; it rested on belief in God. It was built upon faith and obedience. When faith and obedience were gone, the temple fell; its treasures were strippd from it and the work of its artists became a shapeless mass.

A heathen nation became the avenger of an angry

God. He administered punishment through the hands of an irreverent host that cared nothing for the sentiments of the Jews. All that the Chaldeans saw in the costly ornaments of God's house was the metal value of the brass, the silver and the gold.

And so, today, it is profitable for us to learn that all the boasted wealth of civilisation is unstable unless it is built upon a moral foundation. The priceless treasures that are stored in the civilised states are unable to protect themselves; art may please and music may charm; literature may delight and learning may enrich; wealth may be piled up in fabulous sums and oratory may weave a spell around ill-gotten gains, but the value of all is measured by the value of the foundation upon which they rest.

Judah fell because it forgot God. The kings relied upon the military strength of which they boasted and which their allies could supply. They felt themselves secure and obedience to God was spurned. When the test came they were helpless, and all the glories that had crowned their days when they found favour in the sight of the Lord and walked in His path vanished when they forsook God.

God's Laws Unchanged.

God is not changed; His laws have not been repealed. Disobedience carries the same penalties now that it did when Hebrew kings were unfaithful to Him. None of the refinements that have come with civilisation can protect a nation from the wrath of God if the rulers and the people disregard the only sure foundation of enduring prosperity, viz., obedience to God. Even a temple, built for worship, becomes a mockery when worship ceases.

The schoolroom may be a mighty auxiliary to the church, because the brain can be made into a great machine tremendously valuable when under proper control and rightly directed. But the mind is no more fitted than the purse to occupy the throne. Brain and money are both good servants, but they have not the qualities that are needed in a master. A consecrated heart can make a splendid use of money honestly acquired, but money, even when legitimately secured, can wreck any life or any nation of which it takes command.

A trained mind can add largely to the usefulness of life when it is under the control of the spiritual in man, but it can wreck any human being, even civilisation itself, if it is allowed to exercise authority.

"For he that soweth to his flesh shall of the flesh reap corruption; but he that soweth to the Spirit shall of the Spirit reap life everlasting."

Every nation of the present day must stand, if it stands at all, upon the same foundation that Judah stood. It will fall as Judah fell if the foundation gives way.

"Righteousness exalteth a nation, but sin is a reproach to any people."

XXVIII

EZEKIEL: THE WATCHMAN

EZEKIEL 2: 1-6; 3: 17-21

IN a very clear and simple way the duty that each human being owes to his fellow-men is set forth in the opening chapters—the second and third— of the wonderful book of Ezekiel.

Ezekiel, third of the greater prophets, was sent to the children of Israel with a message; he was commissioned watchman to the House of Israel and his duty was defined. He was told what to say and informed that he would share the guilt of those whom he failed to warn, but that he could maintain his innocence if he delivered the needed warning, even though the warning was not heeded.

The evasive question asked by Cain, "Am I my brother's keeper?" has been asked in every generation since, not so often by those guilty of aggressive attack upon the brother as by those who find in the question an excuse for not aiding a fellow being when in need.

An Important Difference.

The matter may be considered from two standpoints. First, one's duty to abstain from injury to another— this is covered by the commandments which enumerate the usual forms of trespass upon the rights of others. The second covers failure to offer assistance when to aid is a moral duty.

The difference between the golden rule of Confucius

and the Golden Rule of Christ brings out this important distinction.

Confucianism was purely negative—Do not unto others as you would not have others do unto you. It simply condensed into a sentence the negative part of the Ten Commandments.

Christ's Golden Rule is positive—" Whatsoever ye would that men should do to you, do ye even so to them."

The Commandments enforce a respect for the rights of others, but there is no warmth or sympathy in them. They prevent injustice, but justice, if it can be defined as the antithesis of injustice, falls far below the standard set by Christ. The world would be a cold place to live in if man knew no higher virtue than justice.

I learned in China that Confucianism did not require one to risk anything to help another. If, for instance, a man standing on the bank of a stream saw another fall in, he would not consider himself under any obligation to help him out; his philosophy did not require that. I was told that some even went farther than that and feared that if they rescued one in danger of drowning they might offend the evil spirit that pushed him in and thus endanger themselves.

It is a complacent sort of philosophy; it not only relieves one of exertion, but saves him from possible risk to himself. The difference between such a philosophy and extreme selfishness is too insignificant to be easily discernible.

An Investment in Brotherhood.

The philosophy of Christ, however, presents an entirely different view of life.

While in the larger sense it is selfish, because it sug-

gests the possibility of one's receiving from another
the good that he does to another—the idea embodied
in the casting of bread upon the waters—still it is a
legitimate kind of selfishness. It *begins by doing good
to others;* it is an investment in brotherhood which
brings a legitimate return.

Ezekiel was commanded to do his duty. He was
told not to be afraid of those whom he was advised to
warn—" neither be afraid of their words, though briers
and thorns be with thee, and thou dost dwell among
scorpions." It was not a pleasant task to which he
was called, but he was to be " not afraid of their words,
nor be dismayed at their looks." He was to set before
them the perils which they would encounter and the
punishments which they would invite.

Then came the words intended for all time; they set
the standard for Gentiles no less than for the Jews:
" When I say unto the wicked, Thou shalt surely die;
and thou givest him not warning, nor speakest to warn
the wicked from his wicked way, to save his life; the
same wicked man shall die in his iniquity; but his
blood will I require at thine hand."

Ezekiel was his brother's keeper in a very positive
sense. If Ezekiel could have saved him by a warning
and failed to do so, " his blood will I require at thine
hand."

A Weak Excuse.

How could Ezekiel escape responsibility? The next
verse tells us: " Yet if thou warn the wicked, and he
turn not from his wickedness, nor from his wicked
way, he shall die in his iniquity; but thou hast delivered
thy soul."

Here we have the two sides of the proposition stated

in unmistakable terms—guilt, if one who can save fails to do so; innocence, if one tries and fails.

Timidity is sometimes pleaded as an excuse for failure to warn others, but the excuse will not bear analysis. We are not timid about other things. We do not hesitate to impart to others any information that we have that would be a benefit to them.

If we see a stranger about to be run over by a horse or an automobile, we involuntarily shout a warning to him. If we saw a burglar entering a house, we would reproach ourselves if we did not notify the owner of the house, no matter whether we knew him personally or not. If we see a pickpocket at work in a crowd, we feel it our duty to warn others who may become the victims; and so it is with other dangers.

In matters of disease we go farther. We not only find pleasure in helping strangers as well as friends to avoid disease, but we go out of our way to tell of remedies of which we have heard. If a new pest appears, everybody tells everybody else if a preventative is found; nothing spreads more rapidly than knowledge of a preventative or a cure. No man would try to excuse himself for failing to give information on any subject of general interest by asking, " Am I my brother's keeper? "

And it is the same with those who warn of intellectual dangers as it is with those who consider the bodily or the financial welfare of others. While farmers are dealing with the crops and the insects that attack them, while the labouring men are dealing with the things that menace the welfare of those who work for wages; while business men are taking notes of the things that make for weakness or prosperity, the leaders in the intellectual world are as quick to hang out danger signals and to spread the news of any new method that promises improvement in teaching.

Why This Timidity?

Why is it that timidity only manifests itself in dealing with spiritual things? Morality is the basis of society and religion is the foundation of morality; why should there be hesitation in speaking to one concerning his soul's welfare?

Is it merely a matter of religious coldness? There are degrees of religious enthusiasm, running all the way from freezing point to boiling point. Those who are just above freezing have no heat to give out; in proportion as one's religion is an active element in his life he feels the spiritual urge that compels him to utter a warning prompted by love and grounded on friendly concern for his fellows.

" We know that we have passed from death unto life, *because we love the brethren*"—that is the test as to whether one has felt Christ's transforming power. And how is this love to be manifested? " Brethren, if a man be overtaken in a fault, ye which are spiritual, restore such an one in the spirit of meekness; considering thyself, lest thou also be tempted." When one is concerned as to his own condition he is naturally alert to the condition of others.

" Perfect love casteth out fear." The danger of being rebuffed will not prevent the doing of one's duty if one has a vigourous sense of duty. Just as Ezekiel was not to be " afraid of their words," or be " dismayed at their looks," so the Christian is called to do his duty regardless of the reception that may be accorded his words. The condemnation of his own conscience is more to be feared than any criticism that fidelity to duty may call forth.

Thus far our text deals with the wicked who has not turned from his way; now it turns to the righteous man who falls.

If, after starting right, the righteous man turns back and dies in his sins, his righteous deeds will not be remembered.

" Again, When a righteous man doth turn from his righteousness, and commit iniquity, and I lay a stumbling block before him, he shall die: because thou hast not given him warning, he shall die in his sins, and his righteousness which he hath done shall not be remembered."

The Foundation of Life.

Those who lay emphasis upon deeds rather than faith accept the Buddhist method of calculation.

Buddhism sets the good deeds off against the bad deeds and makes the accumulated merit a matter of mathematics. The good deeds must outweigh the bad deeds; the account can be cast up at the end of each day or week or year. If the good exceeds the evil, there is a balance to go on; if the evil exceeds the good, the balance is on the wrong side of the ledger.

Neither Christianity nor Judaism countenances the elimination of faith; it is the foundation upon which life is built. If one sins and repents, his sins are forgiven; they are blotted out and he begins life anew. By the same rule, if the righteous man turns back to sin, his good works are blotted out. It is the *direction* in which one is going that counts, not the *distance* that he has gone.

If a man is born again, turns his face toward heaven

and travels straight forward, nothing in the past can mar his progress; and so, if one turns his back on God and travels towards perdition, no good that he has done in the past can save him.

Experience Proves God's Goodness.

One phrase of these two verses has excited criticism —" and I lay a stumbling block before him."

Some who assume to have a more delicate sense of justice than the Bible's God are very much shocked at the thought of God laying a stumbling block in one's way. They take the words out of their connection and refuse to consider the context. The beginning of the sentence reads, " Again, when a righteous man doth *turn from his righteousness* and *commit iniquity.*"

God does not lay a stumbling block in the way of the righteous; it is in the way of the *wicked* that He lays a stumbling block.

In the administration of justice human governments do the same thing. If a government attempted to lead an *honest* man into crime, it would be subjected to just criticism, but when the government lays a stumbling block in the path of the wicked it is aiding in the administration of justice. If one decides to " turn from his righteousness and commit iniquity," he has no reason to complain of a stumbling block that entraps him.

Those who defend the wicked to the extent of criticising the stumbling blocks are much in the position of the friends of criminals who become indignant when the government entraps those who are engaged in the violation of the law.

It is not necessary that a man who *does not believe in God* shall be convinced of the justice of the Almighty. The goodness of God need not be established by proof offered before a biased tribunal; " no thief ever felt the halter draw with good opinion of the law "; God's goodness is proven by *experience*—" taste and see that the Lord is good."

Those who commit their way to Him and conform to His laws will have no reason to complain of either His justice or His mercy.

XXIX

DANIEL: THE DAUNTLESS

DANIEL 6: 16-23

ERE we have one of the Bible stories with which the young are most familiar. The child early learns the difference between the domestic and the ferocious animals. The puppy and the kitten are its first pets, while the lion and the tiger are the first to arouse its sense of fear. It is easy to understand, therefore, how Daniel's thrilling experience in the lions' den grips the child's imagination and arouses its interest.

The lesson of moral courage drawn from it has played an important part in the lives of all who have ever attended Sunday School or studied the Bible under the instruction of parent or pastor. "Dare to be a Daniel" has echoed in millions of little hearts and has called innumerable hosts to courageous resistance in hours of trial.

And its lesson is for adults as well as for youth. There is no day in life between the cradle and the grave when one may not be called to meet a trial in which his faith can be strengthened by a recollection of Daniel's fidelity to God and by God's reward of that fidelity.

A Tribute to Daniel's Worth.

The story as related in the sixth chapter of Daniel exhibits unregenerate human nature and kingly weakness as well as a sublime faith.

204

Darius, conqueror of Babylon, had conferred high authority upon Daniel. We read that immediately after the slaying of Belshazzar on the night of his infamous feast and the ascension of Darius to the throne, " it pleased Darius to set over the kingdom an hundred and twenty princes . . . and over these three presidents, of whom Daniel was first." To emphasise still more the respect shown for Daniel, it is stated that he " was preferred above the presidents and princes, because an excellent spirit was in him."

Such is the tribute paid to Daniel's worth. It is not surprising that such preference, shown to one of foreign blood, especially to one who was brought into the country as a captive, should arouse the envy of his associates. The presidents and princes sought to find occasion against Daniel. Those who deny the fall of man and contend that human history proves continuous progress upward is the natural course, will have difficulty in explaining the tendency of man to sin.

The Bible gives abundant evidence of the fatal malady of sin from the first page to the last, and the record since those days has been in line with Bible history—sin always and sin everywhere. The spiritual nature is in constant combat with the downward tendency. Just as the spark of life continually battles against the forces that would draw the body back to the dust from which it came, so the spiritual in man is battling every moment against the gravitation that, in the moral world, pulls man sinward.

Plotting Daniel's Ruin.

These enemies of a godly man plotted his ruin. The mental machine called the mind, which some are wont to worship as if it were a god, is but a tool in the

control of man's will. It plots a murder as willingly
as it plans a noble service. The wicked hearts of Daniel's wicked associates were in control of their brains
and they succeeded in devising a scheme for Daniel's hurt.

They could not find aught against his conduct in
office, " forasmuch as he was faithful, neither was
there any error or fault found in him." They con-
fessed this; then they said: " We shall not find any
occasion against this Daniel except we find it against
him concerning the law of his God."

What a wonderful tribute to an upright man! What
greater praise could evil men give to a servant of God?

So they set out to snare him through his very loyalty
to Jehovah. And here we see how they employed the
vanity of a king to aid their conspiracy.

They conceived the idea of flattering Darius by pro-
posing a decree according to which no one would be
permitted to ." ask a petition of any God or man for
thirty days, save of thee, O king." And they presented the suggestions as coming from " all the presidents of the kingdom, the governors, and the princes,
the counselors and the captains "—thus including Daniel himself. A lie, of course, but it had the effect that
they intended. The king was weak enough to sign the
decree; thus the trap was set and then it was sprung.

Why There Are So Few Daniels.

They knew that Daniel prayed three times a day and
they knew that he prayed with his windows open
toward Jerusalem where his devotions could be observed by passersby. They were not long in securing
the needed proof, for Daniel did not falter for a moment. He prayed as usual and he prayed with full

knowledge of the decree and knowing that it was to be used against him.

Why, it has often been asked, did Daniel expose himself to danger unnecessarily? Why did he invite punishment when it was so easy to pray in some other part of the room? Why, when he knew that the decree was signed, did he insist on kneeling in front of the window where his disobedience would be observed by any passerby?

Many a Christian has asked similar questions on similar occasions and made an answer quite different from the answer made by Daniel—and, therefore, history does not give us as many Daniels as there should have been.

The effect of Daniel's fidelity can be estimated better today than it could have been when Daniel was praying. His decision, which at that time seemed of little importance to any one save Daniel, stands out today as epoch-making, showing how impossible it is for a human being to calculate the infinite consequences of a single act. The Christian cannot turn out his light for a moment; he must always be on his guard lest an opportunity for service pass unimproved.

"For He Is the Living God."

Let us see what followed. Daniel's disobedience was at once made known to the king, and then the king was weighed in the balance and found wanting. Instead of refusing to be a party to a foul crime, he allowed the conspirators to hold him to a decree obtained by deliberate deception, and Daniel was cast into the lions' den.

Then what? The king spent a sleepless night, while Daniel was at ease among the beasts whose ferocity

was restrained by their Maker. The monarch hastened
to the den at dawn and " cried with a lamentable voice
unto Daniel." Even during the night watches he had
hoped that Daniel's God would save him from the
hunger of the beasts (and from the king's weakness),
and he was overjoyed when the prophet answered : " O
king, live forever. My God hath sent his angel, and
hath shut the lions' mouths, that they have not hurt
me : forasmuch as before him innocency was found
in me."

And then what ? The king had the accusers of
Daniel cast into the den ; retribution followed, as retribution always follows.

And then ? King Darius wrote unto all peoples,
nations, and languages that dwelt in all the earth and
made a decree that in every dominion of his kingdom
men tremble and fear before the God of Daniel, " for
He is the living God."

And then ? The release of the children of Israel and
their return from exile.

An Act That Has Shaped the Centuries.

As it is impossible to foresee the good that may
follow from a single act of obedience to God, so it is
impossible to calculate all the evils that may follow in
the train of a single sin. We know what Daniel's faith
has meant to millions, but we cannot estimate the
calamities for which he would have been responsible if,
in this moment of trial, he had surrendered to the
promptings of worldly prudence.

One recalls in this connection the words of Wendell
Phillips : " How prudently most men sink into nameless
graves, while now and then a few forget themselves
into immortality." Daniel forgot himself into immor-

tality, just as many have done who have followed in his steps and obeyed without thought of consequences to themselves.

Phillips' language is a paraphrase of Christ's words: "For whosoever will save his life shall lose it: but whosoever will lose his life for my sake, the same shall save it."

It is by attempting the impossible that we learn what faith can accomplish; those who lack faith cannot know because they do not try. A coloured preacher once expressed his idea of faith as "willingness to do what God tells us to do without asking any questions." To illustrate, he said, "If God tells me to butt my head through a stone wall, I butt—that is my part; going through the wall is God's part."

Daniel obeyed; he attempted what seemed impossible and by his faith, set in motion a train of circumstances which still profoundly impress the life of the centuries.

XXX

CYRUS: THE FRIEND OF JUDAH

JEREMIAH 29:10; EZRA 1:1-8, 11

THE fulfillment of a famous prophecy, the generous act of a great king in obedience to a summons from the Almighty, and the return of the children of Israel to their home land after an exile of seventy years in Babylon, whither they had been carried captives of war by Nebuchadnezzar—these give us our theme for this chapter.

What was this famous prophecy? "For thus saith the Lord," wrote the prophet Jeremiah from the ruins of Jerusalem to them that had been carried away captives, "That after seventy years be accomplished at Babylon I will visit you, and perform my good word toward you, in causing you to return to this place."

How did God cause this prophecy by one of His servants to be fulfilled? It is told plainly and simply in the first chapter of the book of Ezra:

"Now in the first year of Cyrus king of Persia, that the word of the Lord by the mouth of Jeremiah might be fulfilled, the Lord stirred up the spirit of Cyrus king of Persia, that he made a proclamation throughout all his kingdom, and put it also in writing, saying, Thus saith Cyrus king of Persia, The Lord God of heaven hath given me all the kingdoms of the earth; and he hath charged me to build Him a house at Jerusalem, which is in Judah."

First, let us consider the phrase, " That the word of the Lord by the mouth of Jeremiah might be fulfilled." A similar phrase, " That the prophecy might be fulfilled," which appears often in both the Old and New Testament, is sometimes necessary to an understanding of the passage in which it occurs.

For instance, take the thirty-sixth, thirty-seventh and thirty-eighth verses of the twenty-second chapter of Luke; the phrase " And he that hath no sword, let him sell his garment and buy one," has often been quoted in support of war, but the following verse explains it and gives to it an entirely different meaning. Immediately following the words above quoted we read: " For I say unto you, that this that is written must yet be accomplished in me, And he was reckoned among the transgressors: for the things concerning me have an end."

Why did Christ advise His disciples that they sell their garments and buy a sword? " That this that is written must yet be accomplished in me." And what was it that must yet be accomplished? What prophecy must yet be fulfilled? " And he was reckoned among the transgressors." The sword was the symbol of resistance to the law; it put the bearer of the sword among the transgressors.

The disciples answered, " Lord, behold, here are two swords. And He said unto them, It is enough." Two swords were not sufficient for the protection of Christ on the night of His betrayal or for the protection of the disciples, but they were enough to bring them within the definition of transgressors and Christ was " reckoned among them."

The above is the construction that Rev. Herbert Booth places upon the passage and this interpretation

is strengthened and confirmed by the tenth and eleventh
verses of the eighteenth chapter of John. "Then said
Jesus unto Peter, Put up thy sword into the sheath."
See, also, the fifty-first and fifty-second verses of the
twenty-sixth chapter of Matthew.

The Greatest Practical Argument Against War.

Both John and Matthew describe the incident in
which one of the disciples (John says that it was im-
pulsive Peter) drew his sword in defense of Christ and
cut off the ear of the servant of the high priest. Christ
rebuked him for this resort to force.

In John, He is reported as saying, "The cup which
my Father hath given me, shall I not drink it?" In
Matthew, Christ uses a terrific condemnation of force
which is a continuing prophecy, continuously fulfilled:
"For all they that take the sword shall perish with the
sword," Christ adds: "Thinkest thou that I cannot
now pray to my Father, and he shall presently give me
more than twelve legions of angels?"

These passages would seem to prove conclusively
that the purchase of swords, advised by the Saviour,
was not with a view to use, but rather for the fulfillment of prophecy. Instead of giving comfort to mili-
tarists, the incident brings out the strongest practical
argument ever advanced against war.

How God Uses Human Beings.

Next, we come to the statement of Ezra that "The
Lord stirred up the spirit of Cyrus." The king was
not a worshipper of Jehovah, and yet he received a
communication from the Almighty.

We are not told the form in which this communication came. In other cases we have read that an angel appeared or that the voice of the Lord was heard, but here the medium through which the communication came is not given, but the message was understood and acted upon. God uses human beings to accomplish His purposes; sometimes they are conscious of the call, and sometimes they act without knowledge of the hand that directs or of the purposes which they are sent to accomplish.

In Exodus we read that the Lord dealt with Pharaoh in quite a different way. Instead of stirring up the heart of Pharaoh to a great deed, He " hardened Pharaoh's heart " that God's wonders might be multiplied in the land of Egypt. It was not, however, until Pharaoh had conspired against the Israelites and directed the murder of the children.

Surrender of a Wicked Heart.

When one deliberately chooses sin and enters upon a career of crime, God knows better than man what punishment will be sufficient to accomplish His purpose and to bring about the surrender of a wicked heart. It required seventy years of exile and captivity in Babylon to reduce the children of Israel to submission; when the work was accomplished and the change wrought, God stirred up the heart of a good king to win immortal fame by a kindly act.

When Pharaoh set out to suppress a race by killing the male children of the Jews at birth, God let him have his way until the slaying of the Egyptian first-born humbled this mighty monarch and then Pharaoh let the children of Israel go. God's mercy is as certain to aid those who do His will as His punishments are sure to overtake the disobedient.

However God's message was conveyed to Cyrus, it is evident that he felt that he was acting under divine compulsion, for in his proclamation he announced that the Lord God of heaven had given him all the kingdoms of the earth. It was an acknowledgment that many rulers do not make; too often kings attribute their power to their own ability and influence.

The Danger of Prosperity.

Before taking up the succeeding verses, a word in regard to the effect of the captivity.

The children of Israel went off after heathen gods; they continually forgot God. The prophets were kept busy warning them that the wrath of God followed disobedience and that punishment was sure. The tribes were rent by jealousies and personal ambitions; and then came overwhelming defeat, the destruction of Jerusalem, the looting of the temple, and the bondage of the people.

Here we find one of the great lessons of history, namely, that prosperity sometimes wrecks peoples as well as individuals, while adversity often restores men and nations through repentance and sacrifice. Man's measurements are often faulty; he rejoices in good fortune only to find that it is sometimes poison to him; and he weeps over misfortune often to find in it a needed discipline and a health-restoring tonic.

When a childless couple, possessing great wealth, adopt some poor widow's child, the neighbours are apt to exclaim, " Fortunate child! " Not always. Anticipated wealth has ruined more young men than it has ever blessed. A widow's son may have a better chance.

The pillars of the church of the state, and of commerce have not, as a rule, been the pampered children of the wealthy; they have nearly all come up through hardship and privations. Hardships and privation confer a double blessing—they give discipline and prevent luxury.

The Double Blessing of Hardships.

Many a boy has found himself after his patrimony has been squandered, but climbing is easier when one begins at the bottom of the hill than when the ascent begins at the bottom of a pit into which he has fallen. As the poet, Virgil, has put it:

> The gates of hell are open night and day,
>   Smooth is the descent and easy is the way;
> But to return and view the cheerful skies,
>   In this the task and mighty labor lies.

The children of Israel had sinned and suffered, and now we see regeneration wrought by bitter experience. They had been born again, so to speak; they are ready to bring forth works meet for repentance. The fullness of time had come and a deliverer was at hand.

Daniel's loyalty to God and the striking evidence given of God's guardianship over him, a captive, had made its impression upon the Babylonian empire and may have weighed largely in bringing Cyrus up to the high task which he performed. The proclamation made by Cyrus included all of the Israelites who desired to return to Jerusalem—"Who is there among you of all His people?" There was no compulsion; if any remained, they were to help those who prepared for the journey back to the homeland. The order was obeyed and everybody was instantly busy, the great day to which they had looked forward for seventy bitter years had at last arrived. Cyrus set an example in generosity that could not but have touched the hearts of the others. He sent for the vessels that Nebuchadnezzar had brought, as spoils, from the Temple at Jerusalem and had put in the house of his heathen gods. Mithredath, the treasurer, had kept count of them—five thousand four hundred gold and silver pieces—and all were sent back with the returning exiles.

An Example in Generosity.

This act stands out in the life of Cyrus as an evidence either of a very noble spirit or of complete submission to the purpose of God. If the return of the holy vessels taken in war was the prompting of his own heart, it showed an exalted character, a character quite different from that of other kings and potentates of that day. If, on the other hand, he recognised this as a part of the command of the Almighty when his heart was stirred to release the children of Israel, it shows how complete was his surrender to the command of the Almighty. And so the exiles set out on their return to their beloved city.

We may not at the time be able to see the hand of God shaping the affairs of men, but it is apparent when we look back over the past and see how all things work together for the carrying out of the Divine Will.

XXXI

ESTHER: THE COURAGEOUS QUEEN

ESTHER 4: 10-5: 3

ESTHER is not the only heroine in the book of the Bible that has made her name immortal. She is not the only woman mentioned in its ten wonderfully dramatic chapters whose life holds a great lesson for men and women of all times and all countries.

Vashti, though her part has been considered a minor one, should not be overlooked, especially in these latter days. She proved that she possessed real nobility; she defended, not the welfare of a group, but all womanhood, and she had no guardian to spur her on by appeals to race pride and by threats addressed to her fear for herself.

We read that Ahasuerus, king of Persia and Vashti's husband, was a typical Oriental monarch, with a domain that extended " from India even unto Ethiopia." It was divided into one hundred and twenty-seven provinces.

In the third year of his reign he made a feast unto all his princes and his servants. He showed them " the riches of his glorious kingdom and the honour of his excellent majesty many days, even an hundred and four-score days." Then he gave a seven-day feast to all the people who were present in the Shushan palace. " Also Vashti the queen made a feast for the women in the royal house which belonged to king Ahasuerus."

On the seventh day, " when the heart of the king was merry with wine," he commanded the seven chamberlains to " bring Vashti the queen before the king with the crown royal, to shew the people and the princes her beauty: for she was fair to look on." But Vashti refused to exhibit her beauty before a lot of drunken revellers—" therefore was the king very wroth, and his anger burned in him."

Then the king called the wise men together and asked, " What shall be done to Vashti? "

A Fawning Courtier.

Memucan, one of the princes of Persia and Media, suggested that Vashti, the queen, had not only wronged the king, but all the princes and all the people as well. Memucan seems to have been the prototype of quite a numerous tribe of which some traces still exist; at least the arguments which he employed have been repeated in modern times. Here is his suggestion to the king:

" For this deed of the queen shall come abroad unto all women, so that they shall despise their husbands in their eyes, when it shall be reported, The king Ahasuerus commanded Vashti the queen to be brought in before him, but she came not. . . .

" If it please the king, let there go a royal commandment from him. . . . that Vashti come no more before king Ahasuerus; and let the king give her royal estate unto another that is better than she."

Self-Respect Above Position.

This pleased the king—he was just drunk enough to listen to such advice—and he issued an order that Vashti should no more come before the king, and he gave her royal estate unto another.

Vashti may be regarded as one of the earliest martyrs to the cause of temperance. Her refusal to obey her husband, when he was merry with wine, cost her her crown, but she preserved her self-respect. She deserves to be remembered now when wives have ceased to be the helpless victims of intoxicated husbands.

The dethroning of Vashti opened the way for the selection of a new queen. Mordecai, a Jew who had been carried away from Jerusalem with the captivity, entered his uncle's daughter, Esther, whom he had raised as a member of his family, in the contest, which was open to "all the fair young virgins." After the twelve months required for their purification, the maidens were brought before the king, and the king chose Esther.

We read that "the king loved Esther above all the women, and she obtained grace and favour in his sight more than all the virgins; so that he set the royal crown upon her head, and made her queen instead of Vashti."

An Infamous Conspiracy.

This brings us to our study proper. Haman, who had been promoted to the chief place under the king, was enjoying the reverence of the king's servants—that is, of all except Mordecai, who "bowed not, nor did him reverence." This filled Haman with wrath and for this lack of reverence on the part of one Jew, Haman decided to destroy all the Jews in the kingdom.

He did not tell the king his personal grievance, but did as the wicked always do, viz., pretended that he was prompted by noble motives. For the king's benefit, as he put it, he asked authority to kill them. Mordecai had concealed Esther's race and the king did not know that his queen was included in the decree. (Haman probably did not know it.) The conspiracy promised to be successful; orders were sent forth to " destroy, to kill, and to cause to perish, all Jews, both young and old, little children and women, in one day."

When Mordecai learned what was done he at once put on sackcloth and went before the king's gate. Esther, learning of his mourning, dispatched a trusted messenger to him to know the cause. He sent word to her, urging her to go in unto the king and make supplication in behalf of the people.

Two Wonderful Utterances.

Esther sent back word that, according to the law, any one presumptuous enough to go before the king without being called would be put to death, unless the king held out the golden scepter, adding that she had not been called into the king's presence for thirty days.

Mordecai then appealed to her own interest; he sent back an answer to her, " Think not with thyself that thou shalt escape in the king's house, more than all the Jews." And then the faith of Mordecai blazed forth, he spoke in the tone of the prophets and warned Esther that if she held her peace, deliverance would arise to the Jews from another place and that she and her father's house would be destroyed. He concluded with a wonderful sentence, often used in appeals to those in authority : " Who knoweth whether thou art come to the kingdom for such a time as this ? "

Esther, strengthened and inspired by Mordecai's appeal, returned an answer that ranks with the words of Mordecai. She asked Mordecai to gather together all the Jews in Shushan to fast for her for three days and three nights; she and her maidens would fast also, and then she promised Mordecai, " So will I go in unto the king, which is not according to the law: and if I perish, I perish."

A Dramatic Contrast.

Behold the contrast! On one side was the chief man of the kingdom, with a decree authorising him to kill all the Jews, and with all the power of the kingdom to carry out the conspiracy. On the other side was a Jew condemned to death and a Jewess queen whom her husband had unknowingly included in the death sentence. What an unequal combat and what a difference in character is disclosed!

The scheming Haman, working under cover and practicing deceit, was seemingly near to a wicked triumph, but he had not numbered the unseen forces—the hosts, concealed upon the mountain top, which form the unconquerable reserve in every righteous cause. Moses declares that one with God shall chase a thousand and two shall put ten thousand to flight. Mordecai was number one, and Esther was number two, in the rival army that was to shatter the plans of Haman.

The Jews fasted, Mordecai and Esther with them. And on the third day Esther put on her royal apparel, and stood in the inner court of the king's house; she obtained favour in the sight of the king; he held out the golden sceptre; the crisis was past—she had triumphed. The king asked what she desired and she invited him and Haman to a banquet with her that day. When the two guests appeared and the king asked what her petition was, Esther deferred the presentation of her petition and asked them to be her guests again on the following day.

Haman, in the meantime, had further occasion to be stirred with wrath against Mordecai for lack of reverence. Unaware of impending peril, he ordered that a gallows fifty cubits high be made for Mordecai.

Something also happened to the king. That night he could not sleep; he spent his restless hours listening to the reading of the chronicles.

It so happened—was it just an accident?—that they read to the king of the act of Mordecai in saving the king from a conspiracy against his life planned by two of the king's chamberlains. In a burst of gratitude he inquired whether Mordecai had even been rewarded. And then it happened—was this an accident also?—that just at this time Haman appeared to tell the king of the now famous gallows that he had built for Mordecai.

When they met they were both thinking of Mordecai, but there was a great gulf between their plans. The king asked, " What shall be done unto the man whom the king delighteth to honour? " Haman, thinking that the king had him [Haman] in his mind, promptly outlined a pompous plan by which he should be clothed in the king's apparel, put upon the king's horse, and crowned with the king's crown; then he was to be taken through the streets while attendants proclaimed, " Thus shall it be done to the man whom the king delighteth to honour."

The Last Act of the Drama.

The king accepted Haman's plan, but imagine Haman's astonishment when the king added, " Do even so to Mordecai the Jew." When was ever mortification more complete or humiliation more deserved?

Haman obeyed; we can imagine how he looked as he conducted the triumphal procession in honour of the man for whom he had made the gallows. When it was concluded Mordecai returned to the king's gate, while Haman "hasted to his house mourning, and having his head covered."

Then came the last act of the drama; the king's chamberlain came to remind Haman of the banquet. The king renewed his promise to grant Esther's petition and asked what it was she desired. She laid before the king the plot of Haman. She assured the king that she would not have appealed to him if the plot had been to sell her people as bondsmen and bond-women, but that they were to be slain. She concluded her petition by announcing that "the adversary and enemy is this wicked Haman." The king rose in wrath and strode out into the palace garden, while Haman pleaded with Esther to save his life.

How changed the scene! Only a few hours before, this would-be murderer of a race was planning what he supposed was to be his own ostentatious parade—in a moment the scene changes, he is witnessing the triumph of the man he would have hanged; then listening to the accusation made by Queen Esther to the king; then upon his knees begging for his life; and then he swings into eternity from the gibbet he had prepared for another!

The Same Moral Always.

Just retribution. It is a simple story of faith rewarded, righteousness triumphant and wickedness punished—a story repeated innumerable times in history with less conspicuous personages playing the title rôles, but the moral is ever the same.

Some boast of reason as if it were fit to sit upon the throne. Haman's reason was all right; it worked perfectly until it came into conflict with faith. Then see how faith towered above it. Reason needs a will and a heart to guide it; faith can use a reason to work out details, but it requires a faith to direct and to inspire. " For we walk by faith, not by sight."

Every one who has an opportunity to render service has " come to the kingdom for such a time as this." Every one who is called upon to encounter danger in the performance of duty should meet the crisis as bravely as Esther did: " If I perish, I perish."

XXXII

EZRA: THE RESTORER

EZRA 7: 10; 8: 21-23, 31, 32

H
E was the servant of a heart dedicated to God. Thus has Ezra come down to us through the centuries—not only as a great leader of the Jews, but as one whose life is a model for all times for those who believe and give their hearts to God.

The great lesson Ezra's life holds for us is abundantly revealed in that phase of his career centering around the second return of the Jews to Jerusalem from their enforced exile, as human spoils of war, in Babylon. Cyrus, King of Persia, successor of the great Nebuchadnezzar, who had carried away the Jews captives, was moved of God to bring about the first return to Jerusalem, and the same Divine influence caused Artaxerxes, "king of kings," to commission Ezra to lead the second band of exiles home.

A Heart Prepared to Seek the Lord.

Ezra is a fascinating character; he was a Levite, a member of the priestly branch of the family. He came from a long line of priests; his great-great-grandfather was put to death by Nebuchadnezzar, and he had a still more remote ancestor in Hilkiah, who discovered the Book of the Law, the basis of our Bible today, after it had long been lost to the Jews during the reigns of their idolatrous kings.

As a youth in Babylon Ezra had every opportunity

for receiving an education, but his learning, instead of becoming a substitute for religion, was the servant of a heart dedicated to God. We are told that Ezra " had prepared his heart to seek the law of the Lord, and to do it, and to teach in Israel statutes and judgments." It was an ambition formed early. As a scribe, he entered upon his duties at thirteen, and it required seventeen years of preparation to fit him for his work.

The world does not change rapidly—in some respects it does not seem to change at all. All through history and in every land we find instances of early consecration to a life work.

A countless multitude of boys devote themselves to having a good time, with seemingly no thought of life's realities; they have no plan and drift hither and thither as some promised pleasure points the way. While this is often the fault of the parents, it is not always so; sometimes the most favourable environment fails to furnish the needed restraint and the necessary incentive.

As time goes on, this multitude divides into three different groups. Some catch a belated vision of life's possibilities and attempt to make up for lost opportunities. Some become habitually worthless and neglect priceless opportunities for service. Still others wander from idleness into crime and end their lives in the custody of society's guardians.

Blame for Wasted Lives.

The blame for wasted lives must be borne partly by society. Even Christians may not be wholly guiltless if they think only of themselves and their own children while those about them walk the way to ruin.

A story is told of a very charitable woman who not only refused to speak evil of others, but would not allow evil to be spoken in her presence. Her children thought one day to put her to the test. By agreement they assembled in her room and one after another began to criticise the devil, just to see if she would permit the censure.

They had not gone far when she interrupted them with the protest: " Well, children, if we were all as industrious as the devil is, we would accomplish more."

Is it not true? If all Christians were as zealous in their efforts to save souls as the devil is in his effort to lead them astray, the number of the lost would be greatly reduced.

But while the many are hard to awaken, a few scattered over the world begin early, as Ezra did, to plan for life. Great inventors often manifest their interest in that line of work while they are children; great business men often indicate a fondness for merchandising; great lawyers begin to prepare themselves for their profession; great statesmen commence as embryo debaters, and great preachers sometimes indicate in their early years the direction in which they travel through life.

Where Many Fail in Good Works.

I know an Oriental student who, when only eighteen, had become so absorbed in the study of government that he left his home with only a few dollars, traveled to a distant country and worked his way among strangers until he finally secured the information which he sought. Then, as the bee carries the honey back to its hive, this student returned to his native land to give to his countrymen the benefit of garnered wisdom and the zeal of a devoted heart.

Ezra's life is one that should arouse torpid hearts from lethargy and put high purpose into aimless lives.

It will be noticed that this man set his heart to do according to the law, as well as to learn the law. This is a very necessary addition to knowledge. Many who know the law fail to live up to it. Knowledge that is not translated into action is of little value.

Ezra carried his plans a step farther; his purpose found a triple expression; he learned, he acted, and he taught. He went at his work in an orderly way; he could not act until he learned, and he could not teach effectively until he embodied his learning in his own life.

Sin the Silent Blackmailer.

Inconsistency between practice and preaching has often nullified the efforts of those who thought to instruct while they themselves failed to live up to the light that they had. A dual life is possible only when one of the lives is concealed; when both lives are known one can live but one life, and that is the lower one. And it must be remembered that a failure to practice usually silences one who might otherwise teach.

Sin is the silent blackmailer that paralyses the usefulness of many who might be towers of strength to the community. Consciousness of secret sins palsies the purpose and weakens the influence.

When Ezra set out with his little band of exiles to return to Jerusalem he stopped at the river Ahava and proclaimed a fast, that they might humble themselves before God, "to seek of Him a right way for us, and for our little ones, and for all our substance."

The fast has long been regarded as a religious rite. It is a temporary turning away from the multitude; it is a short journey into the wilderness—a communion with God. It is a suppression of that which is most natural—the appetite—that we may open our hearts to the supernatural. Every Christian might well have his river Ahava where he stops a while to fast and pray.

"The Hand of Our God."

When Ezra appeared before the king he expressed his confidence in God so strongly that he felt it inconsistent to ask for the armed guards that the king would willingly have provided for the expedition. He says: "For I was ashamed to require of the king a band of soldiers and horsemen to help us against the enemy in the way; because we had spoken unto the king, saying, The hand of our God is upon all them for good that seek him. But his power and his wrath is against all them that forsake him."

But the same confidence that led him to be almost boastful before Artaxerxes sustained him on the journey. After they had fasted and prayed they started on their journey, trusting in God to guard them from enemies, and their trust was rewarded. Ezra took his little band through a hostile country infested by robbers and none molested him.

The unbeliever may speculate as to the reasons that accounted for Ezra's security; he may guess that the robbers were busy plying their profession along some other highway, but Ezra gave credit to Jehovah. "The hand of our God was upon us, and He delivered us from the hand of the enemy, and of such as lay in wait by the way. And we came to Jerusalem."

Faith That Unlocks the Future.

Here is another lesson of faith—a faith that unlocks the future to those who possess it. Ezra's faith blossomed early, long before reason could have been of much aid to him. His faith led him to seek to know the law of the Lord, and to do it, and to teach it. This faith developed in him a life that impressed a king and a life that furnished leadership for an expedition.

Eight hundred miles Ezra led his followers through the desert from the Euphrates to their own land. It was in the spring and the flowers of the desert cheered the travelers as they journeyed—the flowers that God has scattered over all of earth's wildernesses as He scatters evidences of His love throughout all the lonely portions of life's pathway.

Never wavering, Ezra completed his journey and undertook the refurnishing of the temple. Only those who believe attempt the seemingly impossible, and, attempting, prove what can be accomplished.

> " Faith, mighty faith, the promise sees,
>   And looks to that alone ;
> Laughs at impossibilities,
>   And cries, ' It shall be done.' "

XXXIII

NEHEMIAH: THE MAN OF PRAYER AND ACTION

NEHEMIAH 4:7-16

WHAT is your talent? How is it being employed?

Nehemiah, cupbearer to the Persian tyrant Artaxerxes, had a talent for leadership; we might call him " a captain of industry." He unquestionably could have used his talent for the advancement of his own personal fortunes had he elected to put it to use in advancing the interests of his earthly master.

But Nehemiah's business was the business of his King, Jehovah. His abilities were consecrated to a noble purpose, and he has given us a striking illustration of the value of talents when employed in work worth while.

Grieved at the news that the walls of Jerusalem were in ruins and the city lay open to its enemies, Nehemiah dedicated himself to the task of restoring its defenses, and, first offering up a prayer to God for help, he begged and received permission from Artaxerxes to journey to Jerusalem for that purpose. He deliberately put aside a life of comparative ease in a court of Oriental luxury to use his talents in an arduous, even hazardous, and unselfish task.

Upon his arrival in Jerusalem, Nehemiah made an inspection of the walls that he might have information at first hand of the work to be done. He went by night from gate to gate without disclosing to the public the mission on which he had come. When he had fully acquainted himself with the task, he apportioned the work among the people, taking care to observe, as far as possible, the local interest that each group had in the particular part of the wall to which it was assigned.

" A Mind to Work."

Nehemiah had so large a part in the work that we may pardon him for including himself in describing what was done. " So built we the wall," he says, and he adds an explanation that is significant—" for the people had a mind to work." There is all the difference in the world between those who go to work and those who are sent to work—between those who are absorbed in what they are doing and those who watch the clock.

Nehemiah was an orator as well as an executive. He had the ability to communicate his enthusiasm to others. He had a faith that stirred to action.

Like the rebuilding of the Temple, it was a joyous work, this of reconstructing the holy city's walls; but it was not destined to proceed without opposition. Sanballat, sub-satrap of Samaria, and Tobias, supposed to be his secretary, first attempted ridicule, and, when that failed, worked up a conspiracy to attack the builders.

No Loafing on the Job.

Nehemiah was a warrior as well as an executive and a persuasive speaker. He gave to his people a splendid slogan—Pray and Watch. Prayer came first, followed by Vigilance. " We made our prayer unto our God, and set a watch against them day and night."

We have no reason to believe that God will relieve us

from the doing of that which is within our power.   A Christian cannot loaf on the job and expect God to save him from the consequences of inaction or carelessness. Nehemiah prayed; he laid his case before God and then proceeded to act to the limit of his own power.

The adversaries laid plans, relying upon their own strength; they boasted that they would take the children of Israel by surprise, but they did not know Nehemiah. He was not the kind of man to be surprised. He did not overlook precautions and then send in an " I regret to report," as generals sometimes do. He armed his people " after their families with their swords, their spears and their bows " and placed them in the open places behind the walls, and then he aroused the nobles and rulers and the rest of the people by his exhortation:

" Be not ye afraid of them: remember the Lord, which is great and terrible, and fight for your brethren, your sons and your daughters, your wives and your houses."

" I Am Doing a Great Work."

Later Sanballat and Geshem, the former's Arabian ally, tried to draw Nehemiah away from the city on the pretext of a conference with them. Nehemiah's reply gives us a notable passage which is often quoted and which might well be used even more frequently than it is. Nehemiah sent messengers unto the conspirators, saying: " I am doing a great work, so that I cannot come down."

A great deal of time is lost because men entrusted with important work spend their time in fruitless controversy with adversaries. Time is precious to those who are entrusted with a high commission and they have no leisure for fruitless dispute. They have a work to do and cannot excuse themselves if they allow an enemy to use time required for work. " Why should the work cease, whilst I leave it, and come down to you? " is the best reply that the earnest can make to the frivolous or the cunning.

Ancient Profiteers.

When the conspiracy failed the people returned to the wall—half . . . wrought in the work, and the other half of them held both the spears, the shields, the bows, and the habergeons." The walls were restored and that, too, in the short space of fifty-two days—a remarkable achievement.

And now for a sidelight on this great Bible character.

They had profiteers in those days as we have them today, but the people were fortunate in having a powerful representative to speak for them and the profiteers themselves seemed to have been less calloused than ours. Although the time required for the rebuilding of the wall was not long, this profiteering interrupted the work of production. The price of food went up and the rates of interest rose. Even five centuries before Christ prices seemed to be exempt from the law of gravitation, the tendency to rise being much stronger than the tendency to fall.

" There was a great cry of the people and of their wives against their brethren the Jews." Some complained that they had to mortgage their lands and vineyards to pay for corn, and that they had had to borrow money for the king's tribute and their taxes. Some had been compelled to sell their sons and daughters into bondage, and it was not in their power to redeem either their children or their lands.

Nehemiah was very angry and rebuked the nobles and the rulers, saying, " Ye exact usury, every one of his brother." He called " a great assembly "; he appealed to the consciences of the usurers, saying: " It is not good that ye do: ought ye not to walk in the fear of our God because of the reproach of the heathen our enemies? " He touched their hearts; those who had been guilty of extortion answered, " We will restore them, and will require nothing of them; so will we do as thou sayest."

Nehemiah's Caution.

At this point Nehemiah exhibits another important characteristic—he was cautious. He was very happy when the profiteers relented and promised to treat the people justly and with consideration, but he was not so carried away by exultation as to overlook the possibility of a relapse. He evidently feared that some, at least, might again yield to greed and avarice when the excitement abated—they might be " bending to the tempest " of his oratory. So he " called the priests, and took an oath of them (the extortioners), that they should do according to this promise." Then he pronounced the customary curse upon them if they failed to keep the pledge they had given.

" The Fear of the Lord."

As is usually the case, there was more in the man back of the speech than there was in the speech itself. Nehemiah had a right to castigate the oppressor because he himself was guiltless.

He held a commission as governor of Jerusalem for twelve years, during which time he refused to accept a salary; he would not eat the bread of the governor,

although former governors had done so and their sal-
aries had been charged up to the people. He did not
do as they had done because " of the fear of God."

He also refused to take advantage of the opportunities that came to buy land when the people were compelled to mortgage and sell it. His hands were clean;
his record was clear. He could condemn and none
could charge him with inconsistency.

Who can calculate the far-reaching effect of a life
like this?—a great executive, a great orator, a great
soldier, a leader trusted and worthy to be trusted, an
honest, upright man. And why?

Because he feared God. He had that sense of responsibility to God that means more to society than all
the laws that man can make. " The fear of the Lord
is the beginning of wisdom."

XXXIV

MALACHI: THE TEACHER OF TITHING

Malachi 3:7-18

MALACHI is numbered among the minor prophets, but the four short chapters which constitute the closing book of the Old Testament, bring us one of the most vital messages we can study.

The burden of the prophet's message was the disobedience of Israel: "Even from the days of your fathers ye are gone away from the ordinances, and have not kept them."

This is the old and oft-repeated indictment, and he holds out the same hope that other prophets offered: "Return unto me, and I will return unto you, saith the Lord of hosts."

After giving utterance to this general complaint, Malachi becomes specific. He employs one of the oldest and most effective forms of argument; he asks questions and answers them himself. The question focuses attention upon the point and the answer presents the truth more forcibly than it can be presented without the question. The interrogation point is like the sign at railroad crossings—"Stop, Look, Listen."

A Searching Question.

"Will a man rob God?" That is a searching question. How can a man be willing to rob God if he has any conception of what he owes to God?

Some men talk about being self-made; question them. When did they begin to make themselves? How did they lay the foundations of their greatness? If any man is inclined to be boastful of what he has done, let him set down on a piece of paper—it will not take much paper—all that he thinks he is, all that even he can consider worth computing.

Then let him subtract that which is due to inheritance and see how much more comes to him by descent than he himself can add. Who would exchange for anything that he himself can do the fact that he was born of a race with centuries of civilisation back of it?

And then let him subtract that which has come to him through the environments of youth—the ideals and the opportunities that have made it possible to accomplish whatever he has accomplished.

When he has subtracted that which has come to him by inheritance and that which he has received through environment, the remainder will not be great enough to flatter his vanity. He will be ready to express himself in the language of Lincoln's favourite poem, " Oh, why should the spirit of mortal be proud? "

And yet, God's children, though the recipients of God's bounty every day of their lives, sometimes are willing to rob Him. Malachi, speaking for God, said to the children of Israel, " Yet ye rob me."

Behold the Promise!

Then he suggests another question that goes to the root of the matter—" Wherein have we robbed thee? " And the answer is, " In tithes and offerings." But behold the promise that is embodied in the following verse: " Bring ye all the tithes into the storehouse that there may be meat in mine house, and prove now herewith, saith the Lord of hosts, if I will not open you the windows of heaven, and pour you out a blessing, that there shall not be room enough to receive it."

Here is our central thought—what are the tithes that we owe to God? One-tenth was the amount the children of Israel were expected to turn into the treasure, a tenth of all their incomes.

Is it practical? Entirely so. Millions have tried it successfully. It is the easiest way to give. One knows just how much he has in his tithe account and his only task is the wise distribution of that of which he is but a steward. He does not have to spend time calculating whether he can afford to respond to requests; he has only to compare the claims upon the fund and this is not difficult when selfish interest is eliminated.

No one is competent to judge in a case when his pecuniary interest is on one side and the interest of others on the opposite side, but one can judge justly and decide wisely when his vision is not clouded by self.

What Tithes Would Do.

Tithes would equip the Church for its work. What would it mean to the Church if it could have for its activities a tenth part of the income of Christians? What is their proportionate part of the total income of the country? A few years ago I had occasion to look up the statistics and found that the country was spending three times as much for intoxicating liquors as it spent for education, and five times as much for alcoholic drinks as it contributed to all religious activities.

There are parts of our country in which there are neither churches nor Sunday schools, and yet the spiritual in man is that which controls and the spirit needs nourishment as imperatively as does the body or the mind.

Christian education is sorely in need of funds. The development of the heart ought to go hand in hand with the training of the mind. As the rudder must be proportioned to the size of the ship, so the moral purpose that directs the life must be strong in proportion as the powers of the mind are increased.

Entwining Spiritual and Intellectual.

It is difficult to estimate the addition to the moral strength of our nation that would come from the entwining of the spiritual with the intellectual in the education of our boys and girls.

We have an influx of immigration from all parts of the world. The blood of every land is mixed with the blood of America and these people help to shape the destiny of the world's greatest republic. Those who are attempting to assimilate and to instruct this new element are woefully lacking in the necessary funds.

In other lands people await the light of the Gospel—wait because the funds are lacking with which to carry the Gospel.

Our nation does more than any other nation for those who live under foreign flags, more in altruistic ways that yield no direct pecuniary return. The Christian Church of America has established centres of civilisation all over the world. While our nation does not claim that its drum beat is heard around the world, it has a prouder boast, namely, that the sun never sets upon one of these centres of civilisation, established by American benevolence, before it rises upon another. But how much more could be done if funds were only available!

Linking Happiness to Virtue.

While duty is the largest word in the language and ought to be a sufficient incentive to giving, still God's Word is full of promises that link man's happiness to his virtue—his prosperity to his righteousness. The first Psalm begins with a lofty appeal to man's highest interest: " Blessed is the man that walketh not in the counsel of the ungodly, nor standeth in the way of sinners, nor sitteth in the seat of the scornful."

The connection between obedience to God and man's welfare is repeatedly pointed out and emphasised. Christ used the same argument in the Beatitudes— blessed, ever blessed, is the promise to those who do the will of God.

And so Malachi represents God as promising to reward those who bring " all the tithes into the store- house." God will " open you the windows of heaven, and pour you out a blessing, that there shall not be room enough to receive it." Who has ever suffered because he dealt justly with God? " There is that scat- tereth, and yet increaseth; and there is that withhold- eth more than is meet, but it tendeth to poverty. The liberal soul shall be made fat; and he that watereth shall be watered also himself."

Contributions and Investments.

Some years ago I was in a party where the subject of giving was discussed. One recalled an instance; he said that he never knew but one man who, in his judg- ment, gave too liberally. The man afterward failed in business, without fault of his own, and was in need.

The person who was describing the incident met this benevolent man after he had been reduced to poverty and said to him, " You are the only man I ever knew who, in my judgment, gave too liberally." Tears came into the man's eyes as he replied, "That which I gave is all that I have left; that which I did not give, I lost."

We get more satisfaction out of that which we give than we do out of that which we spend on ourselves. Our contributions are our investments and the dividends that they earn are large and unfailing—they grow with the years.

There is a moral philosophy that cannot be ignored if one would measure life in a large way, viz., that giving is necessary to spiritual growth, and that spiritual growth is necessary to wise living.

When we give because we ought to give—because the conscience requires it—we do unselfish things that we would not do if, in each case, we stopped to calculate the probable profit before giving.

An Overflowing Spring.

The Christian life is best described as an overflowing spring that pours forth because it can and rejoices in its ability to give. Tolstoy has added a thought to this illustration; he says the spring does not ask where its waters go, but that, as a matter of fact, the waters sink into the first thirsty ground they find.

Water is inanimate and though its ripples seem like laughter, it is unconscious of the happiness it gives. But man can find in giving a real delight, for he has not only the consciousness of duty done but the gratitude of those who benefit by his bounty.

"Will a man rob God?" "Bring ye all the tithes into the storehouse, that there may be meat in mine house, and prove me now herewith, saith the Lord of hosts."

Printed in the United States of America